PRAISE FOR
THE ENERGY BOOK

"I got to know Richard years ago as someone who can genuinely inspire people in the areas of personal happiness and energy. He continues to do this with everybody he meets."

Dick Mecklenfeld, Managing Director, Hot Item

"I've known Richard and hired him to help my teams for more than 15 years. Without fail, after every interaction with him I feel an increased level of energy and enthusiasm in the teams and results improve. He truly understands this subject."

Willem van Enter, Vice President, EMEA OutSystems

"Richard's passion for unleashing potential, combined with his extensive business experience, has significant impact for individuals, teams and organizations. It's always hugely energizing working with him."

Bert Boers, Regional Vice President, SAS Institute

"After talking about writing this book for a long time, finally Richard has made it happen. I'm very pleased for him and for all who will read it and experience the benefits. High energy levels are essential to unleash more potential."

Arno Diepeveen, Founder and Owner, Royal Dutch Sales

THE ENERGY BOOK

50 WAYS TO BOOST YOUR ENERGY IN WORK AND LIFE

RICHARD MADDOCKS

Published by
LID Publishing Limited
The Record Hall, Studio 204,
16-16a Baldwins Gardens,
London EC1N 7RJ, UK

info@lidpublishing.com
www.lidpublishing.com

A member of:

BPR

Business Publishers Roundtable

www.businesspublishersroundtable.com

© Richard Maddocks, 2019
© LID Publishing Limited, 2019
Reprinted in 2019

Printed in the Czech Republic by Finidr

ISBN: 978-1-912555-35-2

Cover and page design: Caroline Li

THE
ENERGY
BOOK

**50 WAYS TO BOOST YOUR ENERGY
IN WORK AND LIFE**

RICHARD MADDOCKS

MADRID | MEXICO CITY | LONDON
NEW YORK | BUENOS AIRES
BOGOTA | SHANGHAI | NEW DELHI

FOR OTHER TITLES
IN THE SERIES...

CONCISE
ADVICE
LAB

SMALL
BOOKS:
BIG
IDEAS

CLEVER CONTENT, DYNAMIC IDEAS, PRACTICAL
SOLUTIONS AND ENGAGING VISUALS –
A CATALYST TO INSPIRE NEW WAYS OF THINKING
AND PROBLEM-SOLVING IN A COMPLEX WORLD

conciseadvicelab.com

CONTENTS

PH – PHYSICAL   E – EMOTIONAL   M – MENTAL   PU – PURPOSE

ACKNOWLEDGMENTS

During the process of writing *The Energy Book*, I realized that many of my insights and ideas have originated through observing and interacting with my family, friends and clients.

They have been my primary source for understanding the huge positive impact of constantly maintaining high levels of energy.

Here is a long and incomplete list of those to whom I am forever grateful.

My family: dear old mum; Christina, my life-partner and best friend; four super kids – Samantha, Julian, Dirk, Jeroen; seven beautiful grandkids – Isa, Christa, Jasmijn, Elise, Emma, Zala, Owen.

Amazing friends: Dominic Cornford, Eric van Paridon, Jon Perry, Nick Matthews, Rogier van Hoorn, Brian Germano, Maks Mulder, Mary Plowman, David Parlby, Frank van Vliet, Coen Bos, Bert Boers, Willem van Enter, Dick Mecklenfeld, Anso Thiré, Simon Tyler, (the late) Chris Dye, Johan van der Waal, Nic Askew.

Each and every one of these wonderful people, and many others, have (often unknowingly) been instrumental in helping me more deeply understand the power of personal energy and how to boost it.

Writing *The Energy Book* has fulfilled the persistent desire to share my knowledge and passion in this area with a wider audience. I would like to thank the team at LID Business Media for helping to make this dream come true.

INTRODUCTION

Congratulations on having this book in your hands. It is a personal handbook containing 50 simple ways to *Boost Your Energy* in life and work.

With all of the daily demands on your energy, finding ways to both increase and better manage your energy levels is not only desirable, it's a must!

I have been working on this for myself during many years, and have discovered it is relatively easy to make happen, something you can do too.

Dictionary definitions of personal/human energy are often expressed as 'the strength and vitality required for sustained physical or mental activity'. And this is probably what most people think about when they consider such questions as "how much energy do I have?"or "how can I increase or manage my energy better?"

This definition is for sure a good starting point. However, when looking at your energy levels, there are actually four types of energy that are essential to review: Physical, Emotional, Mental, Purpose.

These four types are commonly represented in the form of a pyramid.

Each type of energy is equally important when considering how to increase your overall energy, and how to manage it better in order to have more impact in your life and work.

Physical is related to the *quantity* of energy you feel
Emotional determines the *quality* of your energy
Mental is concerned with how well you can *focus* your energy
Purpose is the key factor affecting the *power* of your energy

To become fully energized and unleash more of your potential, it is important to identify and consistently practice things that increase and maintain the levels of each of your four types of energy. When you are able to do this, you will be more fulfilled, energized and effective in all aspects of your life.

You can best build your energies from the bottom of the pyramid upwards. It's easier to increase your Emotional Energy when your Physical Energy is high; you can strengthen your Mental Energy more effectively when your Emotional Energy is in good shape, and so on.

However, the force of your energies works from the top down. When Purpose Energy is strong, this gives additional power to your Mental, Emotional and Physical Energies and thus provides more impact (see *Energy Booster 16*, *The Power of Purpose*).

Let me explain this further by looking at each of the four types of energy in more detail.

Physical Energy: We all need nutrition, exercise, sleep and relaxation. It is part of the human condition. Each of these components provides an essential contribution in building a solid base to enable other types of energy to increase and be used effectively.

Emotional Energy: Most people tend to perform best when they feel emotionally strong and are emotionally well balanced. This is much easier when your Physical Energy is high. Emotional strength and balance is achieved when you consistently recharge your positive energy by identifying things that boost your Emotional Energy, and those that drain it. Simple approaches can then be implemented to plug your energy leaks and focus on the positive aspects.

Mental Energy: When your level of Emotional Energy is good, it is easier to build and manage your Mental Energy. You think more clearly and logically, and your thoughts are less disturbed by the noise and interference of negative emotions. You can then more easily keep distractions and interruptions to a minimum, thereby enabling you to fully focus and concentrate on what you are busy with.

Purpose Energy: When your everyday life and activities are consistent with what really matters to you and what you value the most, it gives you a sense of meaning and purpose. This in turn enables you to focus better, you experience more positive emotional energy, you demonstrate greater perseverance and feel physically energized. Increasing Purpose Energy requires you to spend time reflecting, to clarify your priorities, and to live your life in line with your core values (see *Energy Booster 50*, *Live Your Values*).

One of the fascinating facts about human energy is you can continually renew and recharge it. This book is designed to provide you with simple ways that help to do this, and to more effectively manage all four types of your energy.

Why is this important?

For many years, I have observed and studied the direct correlation between the amount of energy people have and their ability to lead fulfilling and happy lives. It is an undisputed fact that when your energy levels are higher, you have a happier and more fulfilled life. You can make things happen the way you would like them to happen, both for yourself and others. You have increased control of all aspects of your life and can achieve higher success, whatever your definition of success may be.

Is there anybody who doesn't want to lead their life this way?

In this book you will find many ideas with which you will feel an immediate connection. And you will be pleasantly surprised how easy it is to quickly boost your energy.

No progress is made though without taking action. As the saying goes: "If you keep doing what you've always done, you will keep getting what you've always had."

Once you have implemented and started to use a few of the *Energy Boosters*, you will begin to notice an energy increase in all areas of your life. You will experience more balance and happiness, along with the feeling that you are prepared and able to meet any challenges that come your way.

But this impact will only be maintained if you continue to practice the things you learn, so that they eventually become good routine habits, like brushing your teeth.

Enjoy the process of playing with these *Energy Boosters*, of becoming the master of your energy levels. Not only is it a fun journey, this process will help you realize some of the positive changes you would like to make in your life.

HOW TO USE THIS BOOK

This book is designed to provide short, easy-to-read, high-impact, five-minute reading interludes.

Each of the *Energy Boosters* or chapters stands alone and they are ideal for reading in separate instalments. Reading and acting on one chapter per week will help you boost one or more of your four types of energy (Physical, Emotional, Mental, Purpose).

You can also choose an *Energy Booster* depending upon the specific energy type you want to increase: in the Table of Contents, each *Energy Booster* has one or more icons associated with it, indicating the energy type(s) addressed in that chapter.

Most of the *Boosters* are designed to provide extra energy. And some of them are focused on plugging energy leaks, to help you stop unnecessarily wasting energy, which leaves more energy to be used for other things.

As with most books in the field of personal development, you will feel an immediate natural connection with some of the concepts, whereas others might not feel right for you at the moment. Let go of any resistance and go with the flow. Take action with the ones you like and leave the rest for another time.

Many of the concepts in this book will possibly be new to you. Some of them are *common knowledge* or just *common sense*. But most of them will not yet be *common practice* for you.

Knowledge gives insights and raises awareness, it is the starting point for change and progress. However, you will only experience the benefits of your knowledge when you take the non-negotiable next step of putting the knowledge to use, in practice.

This is why each of the 50 *Energy Boosters* contains suggested actions, ideas and simple easy-to-implement exercises which, when practiced on a regular basis, will become *common practices* or good habits for you.

MY SUGGESTION FOR USING THIS BOOK IS TO CHOOSE ONE OF THE FOLLOWING APPROACHES:

- Read it sequentially, one *Energy Booster* per week, and work on implementing the suggested actions during that week
- Read it sequentially and mark the pages that resonate with you, and then execute the actions when you are ready
- Randomly open the book and work with the *Energy Booster* from that chapter
- Browse the *Energy Booster* titles and read the ones that grab you
- Choose an *Energy Booster* by energy type, using the icons in the Table of Contents

I strongly encourage you to keep this book with you, close to hand. So you can (re-)read a chapter during a coffee or lunch break (or 'renewal break' – see *Energy Booster 1*), maybe share and discuss one of the *Boosters* with another person. And then immediately start to practice the suggested actions to help you renew and recharge your energies.

Whichever way you choose to use this book, enjoy the *Energy Boosters* and challenge yourself to be driven to take action. You will be delighted with the results.

ENERGY
BOOSTERS

1. RECHARGE YOUR BATTERY

	NEGATIVE ENERGY	POSITIVE ENERGY
HIGH ENERGY	SURVIVAL ZONE	PERFORMANCE ZONE
LOW ENERGY	BURNOUT ZONE	RENEWAL/RECOVERY ZONE

Your smartphone has a rechargeable battery. What happens if you don't recharge it on a regular basis? Of course, it runs down and eventually stops working. Fortunately, you get some warning messages when the battery level is low so that you can take action and recharge it.

Your body and mind work in the same way. As I mentioned in the introduction to this book, there are four types of human energy: physical, emotional, mental, purpose. And it is absolutely essential that you recharge/renew each of these energies on a daily basis.

If you don't, after a period of time everything in your system starts to work less well. When this goes on for too long, you can even find yourself in a burnout situation. Your energies are literally exhausted.

People often don't recognize or act upon the early warning signals: frequently feeling physically tired, being increasingly irritated and frustrated, less able to focus and concentrate, 'just doing' without a sense of purpose.

The Energy Zone Matrix provides a simple way of helping you to understand this better. There are four zones: performance, renewal, survival, burnout. Think about the percentage of time you spent in each zone during the last week. Write your thoughts down.

The absolute ideal would be if you spent all of your time shared across the performance and renewal zones. I imagine this is not the case for you, as indeed it isn't for me either. In general, most people spend too much time in the survival zone.

The way to change this is to focus on increasing the amount of time you spend in the renewal zone. By doing so, you will also be able to spend more time in the Performance Zone and less time in the other two zones. To increase renewal zone time at work, it's important to take a short break at least every 90 minutes, and do one or more of the following:

- Walk in the fresh air (5-15 minutes)
- Grab a coffee/tea/water and have a 'small-talk' conversation with a colleague (5-10 minutes)

- Put your feet up on the desk and daydream
  (5-10 minutes)
  (don't try to find solutions to problems, just let your mind wander)
- Go to a stairwell and walk/run up and down the stairs
  (5 minutes)
- Watch some Energizing Images ... see Booster 34
  (5-10 minutes)
- Do some belly-breathing ... see Booster 15 (1-5 minutes)
- Do some push-ups against a wall (1 minute)
- Do some tension-releasing exercises ... see Boosters 38 and 39 (1-10 minutes)
- Spend time reflecting upon your 'Life Purpose' ...
  see Booster 16 (15 minutes)
- Call a good friend and have a light-hearted chat
  (5-10 minutes)
- Play some music ... see Booster 47 (5-10 minutes)
- Eat something healthy every 2-3 hours ... see Booster 11

I'm sure you will find many other things you can do to give yourself a short renewal break. When you do these sorts of things every day, several times per day, you will feel much more energized throughout the whole day ... and your performance will increase.

2. ENERGY AUDIT

This Booster is going to give you food-for-thought to better manage and increase the level of each of the four types of your energy. In order to manage your energy levels, it's important to assess their current status. So, let's measure your current energy levels on a scale of 1 to 4.

PHYSICAL ENERGY
Physical energy is related to the quantity of energy you have:

    1 = between empty and ¼ empty
    2 = between ¼ empty and ½ full
    3 = between ½ full and ¾ full
    4 = between ¾ full and completely full

What is your level at the moment?

EMOTIONAL ENERGY

This is concerned with the quality of your energy:

    1 = mainly negative thoughts/feelings/mood
    2 = more negative than positive
    3 = more positive than negative
    4 = mainly positive

What score would you give yourself today?

_____

MENTAL ENERGY

Mental energy describes how well you can focus your mind and concentrate on what you are doing or what is happening in the present moment:

    1 = fully scattered
    2 = more scattered than focused
    3 = more focused than scattered
    4 = fully focused (laser-style!)

What is your current mental energy score?

_____

PURPOSE ENERGY

When we think about this type of energy, the primary consideration is how committed and engaged you feel towards everything you are doing in life:

1 = totally uncommitted/unengaged
2 = more uncommitted than committed
3 = more committed than uncommitted
4 = totally committed/engaged

How would you rate your purpose energy level?

_____

Now add the four scores together to give a total energy level.

_____

If your score is 13 or more, you're clearly in what we call a fully energized state. Your energy management skills are excellent, and your level of energy is sufficient to enable you to fully utilize your talents and skills.

A score of 10-12 indicates that you are well-energized. Your energy management skills are high, but not sufficient to fully utilize your talents and skills. It would be good to work on expanding your level of energy.

With a score of 8 or 9, you are averagely energized. You have obstacles stopping you from fully utilizing your talents and skills. To perform better, it would be good to significantly strengthen your energy management skills.

If your score is less than 8, we say you are poorly energized. Your level of energy significantly undermines your ability to fully utilize your talents and skills. When levels of energy such as this persist over time, your health, happiness and productivity can be seriously impacted. If left unchanged this can lead to a 'burnout'.

Whatever your total score, the suggested energy action is to review your four individual scores and reflect upon how you might increase them.

What specific actions could you take to increase each one of your energy level scores by 1 point?

I recommend you conduct this energy audit once every few months.

3. WAKING UP

How do you wake up in the morning?

Are you like a coiled spring that leaps out of bed with a feeling of: Wow, it's great to be alive! Another whole new day ahead to enjoy and make things happen the way I want them to.

Or do you have to drag yourself out from under the sheets, with a bit of a heavy feeling, and the thought of: Here we go again, another day to struggle through.

I suspect, like most people, you're somewhere in the middle of these two scenarios.

I'd like to ask you the question: wouldn't you like to be more like the coiled-spring type? Full of optimism, energy and *joie de vivre*?

Surely you didn't say no to this?

If you did, I suggest you stop reading now. You probably need to start looking for a therapist rather than reading these Energy Boosters!

For those of you that said YES, let me suggest the following:

Every day, as you start to wake up, before you open your eyes, plant a strong positive thought in your mind, like:

- "I'm going to really enjoy today, whatever happens"
- "Today I'm going to do my absolute **best** in everything I do"
- "Everybody I meet today is going to get lots of positive energy from me"
- "Today is the most important day of my life"

The list of options is endless.

I can't imagine you ever wake up thinking: "I hope I have a really crap day today." Of course you don't. But if you don't give yourself a positive kick-start to the day, you're leaving it up to chance.

THE SUGGESTED ENERGY ACTION IS:

Choose one or two thoughts that work for you and focus on them every single day, before you open your eyes.

I guarantee that then, when you get out of bed, you'll feel a strong urge to rise and shine ... and you'll have a stimulating and energizing day.

4. SIX MAGIC WORDS

"I think therefore I am." I'm sure you've heard this statement before.

It is attributed to the 17th century French philosopher René Descartes. Ever since that time, philosophers and scientists have debated the validity of his words, although they've never been able to reach agreement.

I don't want to introduce a philosophical discussion about this. Instead, I want to share six magic words that can potentially change your life:

"I become what I think about"

You might be interested to know that these words are as old as the hills. As far back as the second century, the Roman emperor Marcus Aurelius was quoted as saying: "A man's life is what his thoughts make of it."

The bottom line is that we, as human beings – that means you too – can change our lives by changing our attitude of mind. We have complete control, if we decide to take it!

One essential fact about this way of thinking means if you want positive results, you need to think in positive terms. Because if you think in negative terms, you'll get negative results.

Remember: "You become what you think about."

I'd like to explain how this works. I'm going to use an analogy comparing the human mind with a garden.

Imagine a gardener has an area of fertile land to make a new garden, and he can plant anything he chooses in this land. Suppose he plants two types of seeds, one of beautiful flowers and one of ugly weeds.

What will happen?

Both will grow equally well. The land is fertile and doesn't care what a seed will produce.

In fact, the weeds often grow faster and, given the chance, they'll choke the beautiful flowers. If you want the flowers to prosper, you need to help them.

Your mind works in exactly the same way as the garden.

It doesn't care what you plant in it – a vision of success or failure; positive or negative thoughts; a specific goal or confusion/fear/anxiety – it's all the same to your mind, all of your thoughts will grow equally well.

What you plant as seeds, your mind will return to you as fully grown specimens, whether they be strengthening positive attitudes, or energy-sapping paranoias!

SO WHEN NEGATIVE THOUGHTS ENTER YOUR MIND AND THESE PATTERNS KEEP RECURRING, THE SUGGESTED ENERGY ACTIONS ARE:

- Change the tone of your thinking, the way you speak to yourself. For example, instead of thinking: "I'm going to have a hard time adjusting to this new situation", replace it with: "I'll face some challenges in this new situation, but I will always come up with solutions".
- Self-inquiry stimulates the problem-solving areas of the brain, helping you to come up with solutions. Ask yourself questions like:
  - › How can I see this in a different way?
  - › How can I make the best of this situation?
  - › How would I feel without this negative thought?

_____

_____

_____

- Access the internet and search for 'positive quotes',
  then read a few
- Write down three things you are genuinely grateful
  for at this moment

_____

_____

_____

_____

_____

_____

_____

_____

- Smile

By doing this, you'll be giving the positive seeds in your mind lots
of water and tender love and care. I promise this will have a strong
positive impact on your energy level.

5. POSITIVE ENERGY CIRCLE

For as long as I can remember, people have been asking me: "How do you manage to be so positive all of the time? Where do you get that energy from?"

What they are hoping to hear is some kind of magic formula, the golden key to the positive-attitude door.

Well of course it's not that simple. There is no one thing you can suddenly start doing that will immediately bring you into a constant high-energy positive-attitude state.

It's a way of life and involves lots of different things.

However, I do have one 24-carat gold tip that comes with a money-back guarantee. It's something that everybody can become expert at, easily and quickly.

It is incredibly simple and yet has such high impact.

It's the power of your smile.

Why is it so simple? Because we all know how to do it naturally, from birth, no lessons needed.

It costs so little energy to smile, you only need to use 17 muscles. Whereas it takes 43 muscles to frown!

Why is it so powerful? Because it creates a positive circle of energy flow.

Whenever you smile, not only does it transmit positive energy to everyone around you, it also generates positive energy and attitude in yourself.

As you've probably experienced many times in your life, the energy of a smile is so strong and it almost always generates the response of a smile.

And that's how you get the positive energy-flow circle: you smile, it gives you and others positive energy. People smile back at you, which gives them and you positive energy … and so it goes on.

Not only can we all smile easily and naturally, but the amazing thing is that every human being has a beautiful smile.

If you want to feel the immediate impact of a smile, try it now. Go to a mirror and smile at yourself, a big wide-mouthed one, experience the positive energy you give yourself when you do this.

THE SUGGESTED ENERGY ACTION IS:

Every time you see yourself in a mirror or your reflection in glass – be it at home, in the office, hotel, restaurant, shop; whether walking, running, sitting or standing – practice briefly smiling at yourself.

This action will give you an immediate positive energy boost. The more you practice, the more you will do it subconsciously to those around you ... and you will consistently create positive energy circles.

6. STOP THE MOANING

Let me ask you a question, and please give yourself an honest answer: "Do you ever moan or complain about anything?"

Of course you do, it's human nature! If the truth be known, I imagine even the Dalai Lama has had the occasional moan.

Why do we all do this from time to time, and some people very frequently? What do we think we'll achieve by complaining?

What I think is that people moan because:

a) they want to share their disappointment and frustration, thinking that something shared is something halved
b) they believe if they complain long, loud and frequently enough, then others may join 'their campaign' and eventually things might get changed ... i.e. those causing the reason for your complaining will change the things that are frustrating you

Let's review the results of these two attitudes.

Sharing disappointment or frustration doesn't lead to halving it, you double it! You pass on your negative energy to others.

With the second attitude – in terms of changing the course of events – it hardly ever has the desired effect. Your moaning inevitably changes nothing.

When did you learn to moan? A possibility is that your parents unwittingly contributed to this process. More than likely they occasionally gave in to your desire for an ice-cream or sweets when you were in your formative years. You started to moan, which evolved into a scream, cry or tantrum until you got your way.

This type of behaviour creates a pattern that gets permanently imprinted in your brain. Which is subsequently reinforced by observing many people around you frequently complaining.

It's a great waste of energy. In general, complaining is an energy leak that achieves nothing.

INSTEAD OF COMPLAINING, I'D LIKE YOU TO CONSIDER TWO DIFFERENT APPROACHES:

- Either change the 'thing' that's causing you to complain
- Or accept the situation as it is and get on with your life!

Neither of these two approaches will be easy. They require discipline of mind and positive energy. But like everything in life, practice makes perfect ... and the more you practice, the easier it becomes.

THE SUGGESTED ENERGY ACTION IS:

- Write down two or three things you've been complaining about lately

_____

_____

_____

- Make a firm decision about each of these things to 'Stop the Moaning'. Either 'Take action to change the thing' or 'Accept it as a fact of your life and move on'

_____

_____

_____

If you do this on a regular basis, not only will you plug some of your energy leaks, you will have a strong positive impact on people around you.

7. YOU CAN OFTEN GET WHAT YOU WANT!

YOU CAN!

Many people throughout your life will tell you: "You can't always get what you want!" ... there are even books and songs written on this subject.

I have been very lucky ... from the day I was born, a wise and amazing woman has continued to tell me: "You can achieve anything you want to." This wonderful person is my mum, who at 90 years old still has that same message for myself and others.

She always qualifies this by adding: "You sometimes have to work bloody hard to make it happen!" But then this is another great value she has passed on to me.

Anyways, I don't want to talk about me, it's you I'm interested in. Are there things on your mind – maybe ones you've even written down – things you want to make happen in your life? Things you REALLY, REALLY want to become reality?

I bet there are, and my challenge to you is: What are you doing about them today? What actions do you have planned for tomorrow, and the next day, and next week ...?

You see, there's one thing my dear old mum forgot to mention: you have to plan to achieve and succeed. Or, as the cliché goes, you'll probably be planning to fail!

Turning ideas into reality is not difficult, but it does require more than just desire and visualization. Because the biggest gaps in the world are between "I want" and "I do".

So, visualize your desire as clearly as possible, believe you can do it ... and then make a plan, to achieve it step-by-step.

Set yourself medium-term goals and milestones, plus short-term actions to get the ball rolling. Then execute the actions and keep evolving your plan by adding more actions.

THE SUGGESTED ENERGY ACTION IS:

- Pick one of your dreams, one for which you feel huge passion and a strong desire
- Make a rough plan with Goals, Milestones and Dates
- Write down the three small initial steps (actions with dates) that will move you forwards in the direction of the goal

Just by doing this, you will feel all sorts of new energy starting to flow.

8. SING YOUR HEART OUT

My daughter Samantha is a singer-songwriter, and I've had the privilege of observing the development of her singing talent for over 30 years.

What has always fascinated me is the amazing positive energy she gets every time she sings, whether performing on stage or just walking around the house. It stimulated me to investigate further.

We tend to think of our voice in a functional capacity: we use it to communicate, to converse and express ourselves, sometimes to entertain. But think about it, your voice is the biggest channel of energy in your body. So much energy flows out into the world through your voice.

When you were a child, your voice was completely natural, you didn't try to 'manage' it. Your voice was pure, unfiltered, often strong and loud.

However, as you grew up and began to consider how to best interact with others, you began to suppress this natural voice in favour of a 'socialized-mind' voice. This 'socialized-mind' voice has more than likely disconnected you from the power and energy of your natural voice. And when you limit and numb it in this manner, you limit your energy flow.

Singing helps you to get back into contact with your natural voice. Regardless of how your voice sounds, you will reap the benefits of singing. We all experience pleasure from sound vibrations as they resonate in our mouth and throughout our body. When you sing, endorphins (the brain's 'feel-good' chemicals) are released, which promote positive feelings and give extra energy. I'm not implying that everyone should seek to become a professional singer, or that all voices are pleasant to listen to. What I'm proposing is that human beings are quite literally made to sing, to use their natural voice in the wild and wonderful ways for which it was designed.

Additionally, singing is an aerobic activity because additional oxygen is delivered to the brain. Which is highly understandable because singing requires deep breathing, which in turn has an immense restorative power, reduces stress and can even put you into a meditative state.

I discovered that everybody becomes more energized and feels happier when they sing. I've concluded that everyone who is physically capable of making sound with their vocal cords can and should sing every day.

SO THE SUGGESTED ENERGY ACTION IS TO SING MORE.

Sing your heart out whenever and wherever you can. At home (e.g. in the shower), in the car, with family and friends ... anywhere where you feel comfortable to do it. Allow your natural child's voice to be free and wild again!

9. THE PACE OF LIFE

Here's a question you may never have been asked before: are you a marathon-runner or a sprinter? I don't mean on the athletic track, I mean in life.

Many people treat life as a fast-paced marathon, to be sprinted through. So they appear to be a sprinter and a marathon-runner at the same time. They seem to have the urge to run and run and run ... not knowing when or how to stop, to change pace, to recharge. They rush from activity to activity, from meeting to meeting ... only feeling fulfilled when they're constantly hurrying, executing everything at the fastest pace possible. And they've always got so many things on their to-do list(s). "I won't be successful if I don't", is often their attitude.

Well let me tell you – whichever way you live your life today – life is not meant to be run like a fast marathon. The basic bio-rhythm of a human is 'Action – Rest / Action – Rest', *ad infinitum*.

It's why we have waking time/sleeping time; day/night; work/vacation; working week/weekend; and so on.

Life is meant to be lived as an endless series of sprints. You put lots of energy into something, run fast as it were ... then relax, reflect, recharge ... and then sprint again.

If you want to experience a long, happy, healthy life, I guarantee you this is the only way to live. Which means applying this approach on a day-to-day, hour-by-hour basis.

So, when you've been intensely busy, for example at work, in a meeting, stretching your brain sitting behind your laptop, or whatever ... once you've finished, STOP for a few minutes, take time to reflect and recharge.

During this brief interlude, before the next sprint, think about what you've just done.

THE SUGGESTED ENERGY ACTION IS:

- Take at least four reflection periods per day for yourself, each one for 5-10 minutes
- Put your feet up and think about:
    - What went well?
    - What didn't?
    - What did you learn?
- What could you do differently next time?
- Feel proud about your efforts, and hopefully the result too

You will experience some remarkable insights, and you will be more energized.

10. 'YES' DAYS

Have you seen the movie *Yes Man* starring Jim Carrey? The story is focused on the main character Carl who attends a motivational seminar and makes a commitment to answer "yes" to every opportunity. The resulting situations in which he finds himself provide valuable food-for-thought, and lots of laughs. The film ends with Carl understanding that saying "yes" to everything is merely a starting point to open his mind to other possibilities. It's not the intention to stop him saying "no" when needed.

I'm not suggesting you follow Carl's example and literally say "yes" to everything. You might quickly find yourself taking on all sorts of tasks that overload your schedule and stop you from meeting previous commitments made to others or yourself.

My suggestion is that, at least once per week, you have a day when you say "yes" more often. There are many ways you can do this without landing yourself in difficult or undesired situations.

FOR EXAMPLE:

- Unless you strongly disagree with someone's idea or opinion, do your best to agree and support them
- Don't constantly get into discussions to prove you are right about everything. Often allow the other person to be right
- If somebody indicates (in their opinion) that you've made a mistake, react with a "mea culpa" or "my bad" ... don't get defensive!
- During your "yes" days, say "yes" at least twice to something you don't want to do
- If someone asks you to do something strange or out of the norm, say "yes"
- Say "yes" to things that will take you out of your comfort zone, maybe things you fear or haven't done before
- When your kids (if you have them) ask if you can play with them, say "yes" ... even if it's just for a short while, unless it's absolutely not possible
- If you want to do 'A' and others want to do 'B', do 'B'
- Try to let your first inner-voice reaction to almost everything be "yes". You can always thereafter work your way back to "maybe" or "no" if necessary

When you reduce the carefully analyzing (or over-analyzing!) attitude to things you're confronted with, when you spend less time disagreeing with people and trying to defend your opinions and ideas, when you strip away the complexity you frequently apply to decision-making ... then your days will be less stressful and you can focus more of your mental and emotional energies on the things that are important to you. All sorts of new unexpected opportunities will appear in your path, and a positive domino effect will happen in your life.

11. EAT LIKE A BABY

We all need fuel to be able to do our daily activities. What is the pattern of your fuel intake throughout the day? Is your energy supply in line with the demand on your energy?

Do you begin the day with a healthy breakfast? Or do you rush out of the door having downed a quick coffee/tea and maybe grabbed a sandwich/cereal bar to eat on the way to work? Do you think that breakfast is for wimps?

The word 'breakfast' originates from the fact that we all need to 'break the fast' after a night's sleep, during which your fuel intake has been reduced to zero. It's often considered to be the most important meal of the day, because of this fact: your engine can't run on empty!

When do you next eat? Lunchtime? Or maybe a snack mid-morning?

The concept of eating like a baby doesn't mean sucking on a mother's breast. It's related to eating appropriate amounts on a regular basis throughout the day, ideally eating something (healthy) every 2-3 hours.

For a balanced intake, it is highly recommended to eat a strategic snack in between breakfast and lunch, and again between lunch and dinner. A healthy snack consists of a combination of protein (for example cheese or nuts) and a fresh fruit, dried fruit, or fruit yoghurt. Or maybe, for convenience, a (healthy) energy bar.

A COUPLE OF IMPORTANT TIPS REGARDING LUNCH AND DINNER ARE TO:

- Have a 'balanced plate', with 25% protein, 25% grains/carbohydrates and 50% vegetables/fruit
- Use smaller plates to make sure you don't over-eat
- Never have a second helping – often a bad habit at dinner-time!

You don't have to try to be a saint and only consume healthy stuff (so-called 'need' foods). If you have the desire, allow yourself to eat some of the less healthy things such as sweets, cakes, desserts, crisps, alcohol, sweetened drinks ... the so-called 'want' foods. The key is to maintain a good balance between 'need' and 'want' foods. A recommended ratio is 70-80% 'need' versus 30-20% 'want'.

I guarantee if you follow these eating principles, you will have more physical energy, and your energy levels will be much better balanced throughout the day. Don't delay, start today!

12. RESHAPE YOUR BRAIN

Have you ever heard of neuroplasticity? It is an umbrella term refer-ring to the ability of your brain to physically change shape throughout your life, through experiences and thinking. The concept of neuro-plasticity is not new and was first talked about in the 1800s. How-ever, with more recent scientific developments provided by functional magnetic resonance imaging (fMRI), this amazing reshaping ability of the brain has been confirmed.

There used to be a commonly held belief that the adult brain was physiologically hard-wired after the formative years of childhood. It's certainly true that your brain is much more plastic during the early years, but plasticity can happen throughout your life. And you can easily stimulate this.

The basic truth is your experiences have a huge influence, not just for how they feel in the moment, but for the lasting traces they leave in your brain. Your experiences of happiness, worry, love, stress, sadness and anxiety have a tangible effect on your neural networks. And the brain-shaping process is especially impacted by your conscious experiences, the thoughts that are in the foreground of your awareness. Simply put, your brain takes its shape from what it focuses on.

There are many ways that neuroplasticity can have a lasting impact. One of them is to train your brain to become more conscious of positive things, thereby increasing your positive emotional energy.

HERE IS A SUGGESTED PROCESS GUARANTEED TO ACHIEVE THIS:

- Buy a small notebook and keep it on your bedside table. Use it exclusively for this brain-training purpose
- As one of your last actions before turning out the lights, write down between three and five positive experiences that happened to you during the day
- Which experiences, however mundane, gave you pleasure? What praise and feedback did you receive? What were the moments of pure good fortune? What were your achievements, no matter how small? What made you feel grateful? How did you express kindness?
- From time to time, read through some of your Positive Experience journal notes

Do this every day for a small number of weeks. You will not only experience a more positive feeling in general, you will also increasingly notice the positive aspects of all sorts of things that are happening in your life ... without even having to try!

13. DRINK LIKE A FISH

The expression 'drink like a fish' normally means to consume excessive amounts of alcohol. Well that's not what I'm referring to here! What I'm meaning is the necessity to drink water throughout the day, seven days a week, 365 days per year.

You may know that 60% of your body consists of water, and your blood is 90% water ... water is literally the liquid of life. Our bodies are constantly losing water through breathing, sweating and digestion. Thus, to maintain a healthy body, it's essential to keep rehydrating your system. Even when mildly dehydrated, bodily functions work less efficiently, fatigue starts to happen, alertness and concentration are decreased.

You know you're dehydrated when you feel thirsty. Another simple test is to check the colour of your urine when you pee. When the body is properly hydrated, the colour should be pale lemon or colourless.

If it's a stronger colour of yellow, your system is definitely in need of more water.

HERE ARE A FEW OF THE HEALTH BENEFITS OF AN APPROPRIATE DAILY INTAKE OF WATER. IT ...

- Flushes out toxins, gets rid of waste
- Boosts your metabolism, helps digestion
- Helps to maintain a healthy blood pressure
- Prevents kidney damage
- Promotes healthy skin, increases skin-elasticity (reduces signs of aging)
- Contributes to a stable body weight

There are many more health benefits, but equally important is that drinking water energizes you, reduces muscle fatigue, increases concentration and improves your mood. You literally feel better.

The commonly recommended daily water intake is between 1½ – 2½ litres, depending upon your body weight. This translates to between six and eight medium-sized glasses per day. By the way, cups of coffee or tea don't count towards your quota, they don't hydrate the body!

HERE ARE A FEW TIPS TO GET YOU GOING:

- Always have a refillable bottle with you – at work, home and play – and sip water throughout the day
- Thirty minutes before every meal, drink one full glass of water
- If you drink alcohol with dinner, have a glass of water 30 minutes after the meal
- Every time you go to the bathroom, drink a glass of water afterwards
- When you pass a water-cooler, refill your bottle or grab a cup of water and drink it
- If you do 'accidentally' drink like a fish with alcohol, make sure you consume at least two glasses of water before bed .... as a hangover prevention action!

When you follow these tips, you will not only benefit from the many health aspects, you will be noticeably more energized.

14. STOP SWITCH-TASKING

The word multi-tasking is often used in a wrong way. People usually mean something different, which is called 'switch-tasking'. Let me explain the difference.

Multi-tasking is when you are doing multiple (connected) tasks, all focused on achieving the same singular result. For example, when you are driving a car, you need to multi-task to achieve the normal desired outcome of getting safely from A to B. This involves many tasks such as using the accelerator/clutch/gear-shift/brakes, checking rear-view and wing mirrors, watching the dials, keeping an eye on the road ahead and other vehicles, reading signposts, etc.

Switch-tasking is when you are busy switching between different (un-connected) tasks that are not focused on the same singular outcome. For example, me working on this Booster, stopping to read an email that popped-up and sending a reply, picking up my phone that pinged with a WhatsApp message and reading/ responding to it, listening-in to a conversation between colleagues, back to writing this Booster.

Your brain can handle multi-tasking. But it doesn't perform very well when it's switch-tasking, and there is a price to pay.

Switch-tasking stops you from achieving a flow-state in your mind. This is when you are able to sharply focus, when you can fully utilize your mental energy to achieve the best results.

A flow-state not only helps you to do your best work and more easily solve problems – your enjoyment of what you are doing increases, because it feels less like work!

Switch-tasking takes more time to complete the different tasks you are attempting ... as opposed to single-tasking, which is when you focus on one task at a time.

Additionally, research shows that it can take several minutes to get back into a flow-state once you have been distracted from a task. Thus, switch-tasking leads to lower productivity and quality, and costs more time. It's an energy leak. It can also be dangerous. An example is when people are multi-tasking driving a car and are simultaneously switch-tasking by using their smartphone! Lastly, switch-tasking increases stress levels.

With all of these downsides, I highly recommend you immediately stop switch-tasking and start single-tasking (or multi-tasking for example when driving a car, or cooking a meal ...).

The main way to do this is to avoid as many distractions as possible, to reduce the temptation to allow yourself to be distracted.

HERE ARE SOME TIPS TO DO THIS:

- Only open your email account at certain times during the day
- Turn off all notifications on your computer and smartphone
- Close all applications on your computer except the ones you need for the task in hand
- When you want to single-task, turn off your phone (also do this in meetings and creative sessions!)
- When talking on your phone, close your laptop and focus on the conversation
- Allocate a block of time for a specific task, and shut yourself away from others (set a timer on your phone)

The more you single-task, the higher your productivity and the quality of your work will be. You will get more "bang-for-your-buck" from your Mental Energy.

SWITCH-TASKING VERSUS SINGLE-TASKING EXERCISE

This is a three-part exercise to show that switch-tasking takes more time than single-tasking.

(use the timer on your smartphone)

> **Task 1:** time yourself saying out loud the letters of the alphabet (A, B, C, ... until Z)
>
> **Task 2:** say the numbers 1, 2, 3, ... until 26
>
> **Task 3:** time yourself saying the first letter followed by the first number (A-1), then the next letter and next number (B-2), and so forth, until you get to the end (Z-26)

How long did Task 1 take? Probably five seconds.

And Task 2? Maybe another five seconds.

How about Task 3? I guess around 30 seconds ... and possibly you made one or more mistakes.

I trust this is proof for you!

15. USE YOUR NOSE AND BELLY

The main sources of life are oxygen and water. I talked about the importance of a good daily water intake in Booster 13. This Booster is about increasing oxygen intake to enhance energy levels in your body.

You know how to breathe, right? Breathing is a 24/7 unconscious act. It provides necessary oxygen to your body, without which the cells of your body would quickly die. But are you breathing the right way?

According to medical experts, most people breathe at less than half of their full capacity. Restricted breathing greatly decreases the respiratory function, which in turn reduces energy levels in the body. Oxygen is one of the primary sources of life and exhalation is the main way to expel toxins from our bodies. Poor breathing can contribute to a multitude of health problems, from high blood pressure to insomnia.

To improve your breathing, it's important to do more nasal-breathing. Your body is designed to breathe in and out through your nose. However, most people breathe a lot through their mouth, which can be likened to trying to eat through your nose!

Why do people often breathe 'wrongly'? Because we are frequently overstimulated and overworked in our daily lives, and a feeling of negative stress is often present. This leads to more mouth and chest breathing, only taking air into the upper lungs, which triggers specific nerve receptors that stimulate a 'fight or flight response' (the instinctive physiological response to a threatening situation, which readies one either to resist forcibly or to run away).

BREATHING IN AND OUT THROUGH YOUR NOSE HELPS YOU TO TAKE FULLER, DEEPER BREATHS. HERE ARE JUST A FEW OF THE BENEFITS:

- The lungs extract oxygen from the air during both exhalation and inhalation. Because the nostrils are smaller than the mouth, air exhaled through the nose creates a back-flow of air (and oxygen) into the lungs
- Nasal-breathing ensures a proper oxygen/carbon-dioxide exchange during respiration, which leads to a balanced pH in your blood. During mouth-breathing, carbon-dioxide is lost too quickly
- Breathing through the nose forces you to slow down the process, thereby reducing hypertension and stress
- The increased oxygen you get through nasal-breathing increases energy and vitality

So, use your nose more!

Now let's talk about your belly. 'Belly-breathing' uses the diaphragm, which is the muscle designed to do most of the heavy work for proper breathing. The diaphragm should rise and fall with each breath, producing a belly movement. This movement massages the stomach and vital digestive organs, which further stimulates the removal of toxins from the body.

Most importantly, belly-breathing fills the lower lungs. This gives a higher oxygen intake and also activates specific nerve receptors that are abundant in the lower lungs, ones that are associated with calming the body and mind.

TO PRACTICE BELLY-BREATHING:

- Relax your shoulders and sit back or lie down
- Place one hand on your belly and one on your chest
- Slowly breathe in through your nose for a few seconds, feeling the air move into your abdomen and feeling your stomach move out. Your stomach should move more than your chest
- Hold your breath for a few seconds
- Breathe out slowly and completely, while pressing on your abdomen – if you find breathing out through your nose difficult at first, then breathe out through pursed lips
- Repeat ten times

When you practice nasal- and belly-breathing on a regular basis, slowly but surely your system will start to do this automatically, without you thinking. This leads to increased energy levels and will have a significant positive impact on your overall calmness and balance.

16. THE POWER OF PURPOSE

Understanding the power of purpose provides essential insights to enable you to use all of your energies in an effective and efficient manner, thereby unleashing more of your potential.

A sense of Life Purpose promotes physical, emotional and mental health. It is an undisputed fact that people who define and follow their life purpose lead happier, healthier and longer lives.

[Watch Richard Leider's Tedx talk on this subject: "How to unlock the power of purpose"]

Not everyone feels the need to be philosophically busy with the purpose of their life. However, we all have a need to contribute, to feel valued, to be needed. And this is what Life Purpose provides.

At some point in their lives, many people ask themselves questions like, "Why am I doing what I do?", "What is the point of all this?", "Why do I get up in the morning?"

In trying to answer these questions we initiate a personal 'project' to find our Life Purpose. But it's not something you have to go out and get. It's something you need to identify and unlock within yourself. It is also not a case of having a purpose, it is related to living purposefully. Living purposefully is about using your qualities and talents to create more meaning and fulfilment for yourself and others.

LET'S LOOK AT SOME DICTIONARY DEFINITIONS OF PURPOSE:

- Something done *intentionally*, *consciously*
- The *reason* you do something
- Somebody who has purpose is *determined*, *resolute*

THUS, A LIFE PURPOSE IS BASICALLY A CHOICE, AN INTENTION TO LIVE IN A CERTAIN WAY. HERE ARE SOME QUESTIONS TO HELP INITIATE THE PROCESS OF IDENTIFYING YOUR LIFE PURPOSE:

- During the last week, which moments gave you strong feelings of satisfaction?
- During the previous six months, when have you felt truly alive and energized, 'in-the-flow'? What were you doing then?
- What are the biggest challenges you have experienced in your life? Which talents and qualities did you use to overcome them?
- How would you like your family and friends to describe you at your funeral?
- Which activities most inspire and energize you during an 'average' day?
- How do you behave when you're at your best?
- If you never had to work again, how would you spend your days to feel fulfilled, relevant and alive?

When you have answered these questions, spend some chunks of time reviewing and reflecting upon your answers. You will begin to identify common 'threads' that lead towards your Life's Purpose.

I highly recommend that you then try to increasingly live your life in line with these 'threads'. You will undoubtedly experience a huge increase in impact from all of your energies, in all parts of your life. Your energy levels will be higher, and you will feel more fulfilled and satisfied.

17. PLAY MORE

How do you feel when you are playing? For example: laughing and joking with others, playing a game with children or adults, busy with a sport, etc.

Most people respond with things like: "I feel energized"; "I let go of fears and anxieties, I go with the flow"; "I live in the moment."

Why is this? It's because when you play, your so-called 'inner child' takes over. We all have an inner child within us, although it's often dormant and buried under the pressures of being an adult. We allow our carefree, light-hearted inner child to be suppressed by the weight of the responsibilities, to-do-lists, accountabilities and the correctness of being a mature grown up.

I suggest it's high time you let your fun-loving inner child frequently rise to the surface. And the best way to do this is to play more ... at home, at work, everywhere. When we're at work, the word 'play' is frowned upon. People think it's frivolous, a waste of productive time. They say things like "stop playing around and get back to work". The general attitude in most organizations is that work is a serious thing!

But if you take work (and life) too seriously, you get trapped in your conscious rational and emotional thinking. You massively restrict access to your creative powers, and you consequently limit the potential impact of your mental energy.

Research shows that playing at work generates increased energy, creativity, excitement and humour. It is also linked to less fatigue, boredom and stress.

SO STOP TAKING YOURSELF, YOUR WORK AND LIFE TOO SERIOUSLY ... BE LIGHT-HEARTED AND PLAYFUL IN ALL PARTS OF YOUR LIFE. HERE ARE SOME IDEAS TO HELP YOU PLAY MORE AT WORK:

- Have toys on your desk and play with them from time-to-time, encourage others to do the same. Yo-yos, spinning tops, juggling balls and so on are great desk-toys
- Laugh and joke. Get a joke-of-the-day sent to your email and share it with colleagues
- In a meeting, suggest that anybody who writes on a flipchart/whiteboard has to do this with their opposite (to normal) hand
- In conversations, sometimes ask the other person to tell the silliest/funniest thing that happened to them during the last week ... and then you do the same

- During meetings, keep a count of the number of times words like 'but', 'must', 'should', 'I think', 'impossible' occur ... and share the results at the end of the meeting
- Occasionally play a practical joke on unsuspecting colleagues ... and be prepared to have one played back on you later!
- Introduce fun competitions ... challenge colleagues to come up with creative ideas in all sorts of situations, or some other type of output-based competition

Being a mature and responsible adult is totally compatible with simultaneously having a playful child-like outlook on the world. Play more and you'll experience it for yourself.

18. MANAGE YOUR EMOTIONS

Emotions are feelings, and fortunately we have them all of the time. They are an absolute necessity to be able to feel alive and experience life fully. Emotions are very powerful: they help you to express how you feel; they hugely affect the way you think and act; and they provide essential information to assist making decisions.

In order to maximize the impact of your emotional energy, it is important to learn how to effectively manage your emotions, in particular the negative ones. And this isn't easy, because emotions are not consciously controlled.

The part of the brain that deals with emotions is the limbic system, which is the earliest developed part of the human brain and thus the most primitive. This is why emotional responses are often primal: they are based upon the need to survive.

Emotions are usually linked to previous experiences. If something has happened to you in the past, good or bad, then your emotional response to a similar situation in the current timeframe is generally quite strong. It stimulates an immediate positive or negative feeling. But your emotional response to new situations frequently isn't directly related to what is actually happening now. Understanding this link to previous experiences is the key to managing your emotions. Here are some simple techniques to help you uncouple the links to your past and have appropriate emotional responses in the present.

LABELLING

Give the emotion you are feeling a 'label', and then speak it. When you describe the emotion in two or three words, it lowers any stress you might be experiencing and helps you to manage your response.

For example, "This feels heavy/difficult/awkward". Don't expand upon this by adding "because ..."! If you do, your negative feelings will increase.

REFRAMING

We can't always change the things that happen to us in life, but we can change the way we view them. When you feel a negative emotion, reframe the context of the situation.

For example, if you make a wrong/bad decision, instead of becoming frustrated and angry with yourself, reframe it in a positive way. Say to yourself: "I will learn from this wrong decision and thus improve my future decision-making."

The negative emotion you were feeling will instantly be diminished.

CHANGE YOUR EMOTION

If you feel a negative emotion emerging in you, think consciously about a positive (unrelated) experience. For example: the birth of one of your children, your fabulous wedding day, a great evening with friends.

A COUPLE OF EXTRA TIPS:

- Think of a (funny) word or phrase like "Total Calm", "Pooh-bear", "Silly-billy". Say this chosen phrase to yourself every time you feel a negative emotion such as anger or frustration
- Force yourself to put a big smile on your face when you start to experience a negative emotion

Many people believe that you should leave your emotions at home when you go to work. This is a crazy idea!! When you suppress your emotions, holding them back costs a lot of emotional energy. And the people around you subconsciously sense what is happening, which generates a negative feeling in them.

To quote Richard Branson: "Engage your emotions at work, your emotions and instincts are there to help you."

Remember, you can always choose and thus change the way you feel. By applying the techniques above, you will not only manage your emotions better, you will be able to use your Emotional Energy more effectively.

19. MANTRA BREATHING

In Booster 15, I introduced you to the benefits of 'belly-breathing', to increase your oxygen intake and thereby enhance energy levels in your body.

Now I want to share a technique that provides all of the benefits of deep (belly) breathing and simultaneously floods your body with positive energy and calmness. It combines breathing with a mantra, the repetition of one or two words.

The first step is to decide upon a quality that is important to you. Something you would like to have more of in your life, a quality you desire to have radiate out from you. Examples of these qualities are things like calm, laughter, happiness, love, peace.

There are two parts to the technique, breathing in and breathing out. When you breathe in, you internally say the first word or syllable of the quality. And when you breathe out, you internally say the second word or syllable. Example mantras are:

Breath in	Breath out
Total	Calm
Slow	Down
Happi-	-ness
Care	Free
Inner	Peace
Laugh-	-ter
Pure	Love

Say the first word/syllable so that it lasts the full length of your breath in. For example, if this is four seconds, then the first word/syllable should take four seconds to say.

Similarly, when you breathe out, internally say the second word/syllable for the complete length of your breath out.

The combination of your breathing in and breathing out should sound like:

"Tooootaaaaaal Caaaaaaaaaaalm"

Repeat this for one minute initially. Your breathing process will now be linked to constant repetition of the quality you wish to increase in your life.

Remember to use 'belly-breathing' and to slow your breathing down.

I suggest you start using this technique in the quiet of your own home. Quite quickly it will become a natural process and then you can take it out with you. Practice when you're walking or travelling (car, train, bus, plane) and whenever there is an opportunity.

If you find yourself distracted whilst practising the technique, don't get frustrated. Just gently bring your attention back to your mantra. To enhance this, close your eyes and visualize the words as you internally say them.

Mantra breathing is an amazingly simple and powerful thing you can do anytime, anywhere. It's guaranteed to boost your energy and bring you into a balanced harmonious state.

Try it and enjoy the results ...

20. MAKE YOUR MOVE

Many years ago, a wise friend introduced me to a simple high-impact method that can instantly change the way you feel. Since that time I have used this method thousands of times, consistently with immediate success.

The underlying principle is that your emotional energy is primarily driven by the way you feel ... and the way you feel is hugely determined by your physiology. Whatever you are feeling is related to how you are using your body: your posture, how you are breathing, your body movement (or lack of it).

Try the following two exercises to understand this better:

EXERCISE 1

- I want you to experience the feeling of sadness, heaviness, somewhat depressive
- Start by hunching your shoulders and slumping your body. Breath shallowly (chest-breathing). Look at the ground, frown, speak quietly and slowly about a recent negative event. Allow yourself to become immersed in the event
- How do you feel? How is your energy level?

EXERCISE 2

- Now I want you to experience a confident energized feeling, lightness
- Stand tall, push your shoulders back and your chest out. Breathe deeply ('belly-breathing' – see Booster 15). Speak loudly and rapidly about a recent positive event. Again, become absorbed by the event
- How do you feel? How would you describe your energy level?

Everybody experiences Exercise 2 as one which provides positive energy. So, if you want to give yourself an instantaneous energy boost, practising Exercise 2 will always do this for you.

The fastest way to change your state is to make a radical change in your physiology. This will have a quicker impact than anything you can try and think yourself into. It's like changing TV channels from a sad story into an energizing adventure.

The best way to practice Exercise 2 is to create a personal 'your move', one which you can use whenever you catch yourself feeling hassled, down, stressed, sad, etc.

For example, my 'your move' is to stand up, have my arms in an L-shape at my sides; then I push my shoulders back, chest out, head-up, put a big smile on my face, and firmly pull my L-shaped arms backwards whilst saying "yes" loudly.

I've seen many different types of 'your move'. For example, people leaping into the air with arms raised to the sky saying something meaningful for themselves (e.g. "I can do it!").

Create your own personal move, and then "make your move" several times each day. You'll be surprised at the immediate positive impact.

Simple and yet so powerful.

21. FIVE FAVOURITES

What is your favourite (work-related) talent?

When I say "talent", for this exercise think in terms of which activity you like to do the most when at work. Which one gives you the most pleasure and satisfaction, maybe excites you?

Write it down.

_____

_____

_____

_____

_____

Now think of four more of your favourite activities/talents and write these down. As you create this list, focus on things you can do/execute, activities defined by verbs, not your characteristics.

Once you've completed your list of five favourites, give each of them two separate scores (range 0 to 10, 0 = none and 10 = huge amount):

  a) Development score: during the previous 12 months, how much have you developed your skill related to this activity?
  b) Usage score: in your current job, how often can you use this skill?

To give you an example of how this looks, here are my five favourites and scores, at the moment of writing this Booster:

1. Presenting/performing	a) 6	b) 9
2. Inspiring and motivating people	a) 8	b)10
3. Writing	a) 5	b) 7
4. Creating new workshop content	a) 3	b) 6
5. Coaching teams	a) 2	b) 5

The point is this: when you are busy doing things you enjoy, you have more energy (see Booster 30). So increasing the frequency of usage and time spent on your five favourites will automatically give you extra energy. And when you develop the related skills further, not only is the development process itself energizing, you become even better at doing the activity ... which leads to enhanced personal satisfaction.

LOOK AT THE SCORES YOU HAVE GIVEN YOUR
FIVE FAVOURITES AND CONSIDER THE FOLLOWING
TWO QUESTIONS:

- For which activity would you like to increase the Development score?
- Which activity will you choose to do more frequently so that you increase the Usage score?

Now the final step: how can you make these two things happen?

To generate ideas for action, I suggest you brainstorm with yourself, with colleagues, your manager ... anybody who might be able to stimulate your creative thinking. And once you have a list of ideas, choose the easiest most realistic ones to start with, then ACTION them!

Repeat this exercise every few months, for the remainder of your working life.

22. WALKING MEETINGS

Walking has long been recognized as an excellent form of physical exercise. It is good for your heart and other muscles, and significantly improves circulation. You probably already know this.

There are many obvious physical benefits of walking, but what you might not know is that walking has a huge positive impact on the functioning of your brain. It increases mental clarity and literally wakes up your mind. Why? Because walking increases the flow of blood and oxygen to the brain. And both of these things are essential for maximizing brainpower.

Approximately one third of the brain consists of blood vessels, which use about 20% of the body's total oxygen supply. Thus, it's no surprise that increasing the amount of blood and oxygen that reaches the brain improves cognitive functioning and memory. And because of this, a surprising key benefit is that walking leads to an increase in creative thinking. Research has shown that up to a 60%

increase in creative output happens during and immediately after a 20-30 minute walk.

Clearly, going for a walk on your own is an excellent activity to do on a regular basis.

However, it's also a great thing to do together with one or two other people, for example with a colleague or customer. Not for a casual chat (although this is good to do too!), but to have a 'walking meeting'. To discuss subjects that need a decision, or when you want to explore possibilities, or find solutions to problems. Our brains are more relaxed during walking and consequently conversations are more open, honest, productive and creative than during sit-down meetings held in an office.

Of course, not all meetings are suitable to conduct during a walk. Sometimes it's useful to have notes, a computer, whiteboard, etc.

My suggestion is that you look for opportunities to have walking meetings with colleagues and customers whenever appropriate. Give the other person(s) advance warning so that they can dress for the occasion, especially their shoes. And make sure you each have a bottle of water and a small healthy snack for the walk.

Try it out and begin to appreciate the many benefits.

If it's logistically possible, walking in nature (woods, hills, seaside, along a river) makes the experience even more positive.

23. LEVEL 4 LISTENING

Did you know there are five Levels of Listening? And each one has an interesting connection to energy, in particular to your mental and emotional energies.

LEVEL 1 - IGNORING

This is of course not really listening. It often happens when you're busy using a computer or smart device, and somebody starts talking to you. You hope that by ignoring the person, they will stop interrupting and leave you alone ... but normally they don't! This costs you energy to resist their intrusion and creates a negative feeling in you and the other person.

So, stop what you're doing, tell the person to go away (your choice of words), that you'll talk with them later, and then carry on with the task.

LEVEL 2 – PRETENDING

You know when you're pretending to listen because you keep uttering sounds like "uhuh, uhuh …". It doesn't cost much energy to listen at Level 2, however it's almost always a complete waste of your time, and thus a waste of your energy. We find ourselves in this situation when we interact with people who have what I call "verbal diarrhea" or love the sound of their own voice.

When this happens, interrupt the person who is talking and stop the interaction. Tell them you urgently need to go and do something else!

LEVEL 3 – SELECTIVE

This is the most common level at which people listen. You hear what is being said, even absorb some of it. But a lot of your brainpower is focused on other things, such as:

"Shall I ask another question, and if so which one?"; "Shall I take the conversation over and start talking, if so about what?" Your mind also wanders to all sorts of other subjects such as your to-do list, what you are going to do later and so on. It is quite an energy-consuming listening level because you are constantly switching thinking. And you often miss a lot of things that are being said.

LEVEL 4 – FOCUSED

When you are listening at Level 4, you are totally focused on the other person … on their words, their non-verbal language (especially facial expressions and tone of voice). The other person subconsciously feels and knows that you are REALLY listening, which gives them a positive feeling, also towards you.

It costs less energy than Level 3 because you let go of your own thoughts. Not only do you hear everything that's being said, the words register much more strongly in your memory. And you are maximizing the usage of your mental energy.

LEVEL 5 - EMPATHETIC

This is basically the same as Level 4, with the addition of allowing your emotions to freely be connected to the other person's words. If they feel happy, a happy feeling is stimulated in you; if they feel sad, you feel their heaviness and sadness.

It's the most beautiful form of listening, especially with family members and good friends. And it fully engages your mental and emotional energies.

To increase your awareness of the five Listening Levels, make a commitment to constantly observe at which level you are listening in different situations with various people. Levels 2 to 5 are all OK to use; the point is not that you should always listen at Level 4 or 5.

But if you wish to manage your mental and emotional energies better, I highly recommend that you frequently practice level 4 listening, and level 5 when appropriate. This will also have a noticeable positive impact on your relationships with other people.

24. COMPLIMENTS

Giving a genuine compliment to somebody almost always provides them with an immediate positive energy boost. But compliments are not only good for the receiver, they also have a positive impact on the giver. When you make a conscious effort to give thoughtful praise and say something nice to another person, it increases your self-confidence and feeds your self-esteem. And so it provides a positive energy boost for you too.

Telling someone you admired the way they handled a situation, or how they had a positive impact on you, is a powerful gift. It's free and you have an endless supply of this stuff. It's important to be on the lookout for opportunities to give compliments. This requires you to constantly look for the good aspects in other people. And when you are doing this, you start to see more positive things in yourself.

Giving genuine compliments also strengthens relationships and increases your leadership and influence. People like to be around others who are positive, who make them feel good. They are then more likely to listen to your thoughts and ideas, and to follow your example.

Often the most powerful compliments are ones that focus on specific details of the other person's actions or character. When you pay attention to these types of things, your words tend to have much more credibility and impact than when you state the obvious.

For example, sincerely complimenting somebody on their appearance makes them momentarily feel good. However, when you say something like: "I was really impressed with the way you spoke up in the meeting and shared your opposing view on that subject. I admired your courage and openness" ... then you are recognizing and complimenting something much deeper, that is related to their qualities and character. This has a significantly longer-lasting positive impact.

So, for sure, give people compliments on their appearance, but don't focus on this. Look for opportunities to compliment them on their actions, character and choices.

Remember though that your compliments need to be sincere and genuine, otherwise they will backfire. False compliments are almost always highly transparent and generate feelings of distrust and manipulation.

I also suggest that you look for opportunities to compliment yourself. At least once per day (hopefully more often), compliment yourself on how you managed a particular situation, how you helped a colleague at work, or anything you feel you did well.

This is not selfish or egocentric, it is an act of self-appreciation and creates positive energy in and around you.

Compliments are not things to be saved up for rainy days. Give them frequently and freely to others and yourself. Not only will you provide a positive uplift to people, you will experience a healthy boost in your own energy.

25. KEEP ASKING *WHY?*

As a young child you undoubtedly asked lots of *Why?* questions, all children do.

"Why do I have to go to bed so early?"; "Why is the sky blue?"; "Why can't I have an ice-cream?"; "Why do you go to work?"; "Why is there day and night?"

The list is endless, it's a language game that children innocently play. Why do they do this? Amongst other reasons, because they:

- are curious and eager to explore their fascinating world
- want to understand things around them
- quickly realize that the more they ask *Why?*, the more they learn

At first, parents are delighted by their child's constant curiosity. However, most parents tire of the relentless barrage of questions, especially the moaning type of *Whys*. Often, they will then respond, "because I said so!" or "that's enough questions for now!"

This in itself has a negative impact, informing the child that asking *Why?* is not always positive. Then you go to school and increasingly ask fewer and fewer questions, particularly *Why?* Because educational systems primarily reward students for knowing answers, not for asking questions.

As you progressed into adulthood, you most probably continued this answer-driven approach in your personal and work life ... which is unfortunate. For sure, knowing answers helps you to pass exams during your student years. But asking questions helps you throughout your entire life.

When adults ask questions, most commonly they ask the *What?* and *How?* types, and not so much the *Why?* If you first ask *why* this will help you to think of more specific and valuable *what* and *how* questions.

I also recommend you regularly challenge your own thoughts and actions with the why question: for example, "Why do I think this?"; "Why am I doing this?"; "Why would I make this decision?"

By doing this you enhance your understanding of why you are doing things and open yourself to the possibility of challenging things that don't fit with your desires and values. This process will automatically fuel your Purpose Energy.

Encourage yourself to adopt the young child attitude of frequently asking *why* in all parts of your life, and especially to yourself. The resulting clarity and insights will be highly refreshing and energizing.

26. HAVE MORE STRESS

This probably sounds like strange advice, to have more stress in your life. Because we usually associate the word stress with negative situations. This leads most people to believe that all stress is bad for you, which is not true.

There are two different types of stress that you experience, Eustress and Distress. Distress is the type that refers to negative stress. Eustress is the term for positive stress. It is derived from combining the Greek suffix 'eu', meaning 'good', together with the word stress. Eustress literally means 'good stress'. Eustress is the positive cognitive response to stress. It is healthy and generates a sense of fulfilment and other good feelings.

EUSTRESS:

- Feels positive, exciting and motivating
- Provides an energy boost
- Improves personal performance
- Creates a perception of "I can handle this situation"

WHEREAS DISTRESS CAUSES:

- Unpleasant feelings
- A depletion of your energy
- A decrease in personal performance
- A perception of not being able to handle a situation
- Anxiety and concern
- Potential physical, emotional and mental issues

Both types of stress can motivate you to change your habits, to help you act in ways that will bring about conscious and meaningful change.

To enhance your energy, your focus should be on avoiding and decreasing Distress, and on finding opportunities to increase Eustress.

Sometimes increasing Eustress can initially feel uncomfortable, because this often requires you to move outside of your comfort zone, to push your boundaries. You might experience a feeling of 'butterflies in your stomach'. But this quickly subsides as you become absorbed by the excitement and energy boost that occurs.

HERE ARE SOME IDEAS TO HAVE MORE EUSTRESS IN YOUR LIFE:

- Reconnect with an old friend or family member
- Learn a new skill or start a new hobby
- Improve your communication skills and put them into practice
- Join a club or community group, to meet new people and potentially provide a contribution
- Work on your physical strength ... set a goal, or train for a challenging athletic event
- Organize a fun outing or vacation with your family
- Improve your health habits (nutrition, exercise, relaxation, sleep, etc)
- Take a roller-coaster ride at an amusement park

Another simple way to increase your Eustress: every time you feel negative (dis)stress, ask yourself what you can immediately change to make this stress work in a positive way for you ... and then take action.

Research shows that both types of stress are 10% caused by external factors and 90% by your attitude. So, remember you (mostly) do it to yourself, just you and no-one else!

I highly recommend you take control and find ways to have more Eustress in your life. You will be delighted by the tremendous energy boost it will bring.

27. MOTIVATION FACTORS

At work, everybody has a number of things that can motivate them further, potentially providing extra energy, so-called (work) motivation factors. We also have a number of things which are important to feel generally satisfied about, so-called (work) hygiene factors. The difference between the two sets of factors is that hygiene factors just need to be OK, they don't give extra energy. When they are not being met, we feel dissatisfied and they generate energy leaks.

Of course, everybody is different. Something that is a motivation factor for one person can be a hygiene factor for somebody else. For example, 'Compensation' is a hygiene factor for me. I need to feel that it's OK, that I'm being compensated appropriately for my efforts. For many other people, 'Compensation' is a strong motivation factor.

When your motivation factors are scoring high, you experience an extra 'spring in your step', you feel happier and more energized.

What are your key motivation factors at work?

> **HERE ARE SOME EXAMPLES TO CHOOSE FROM:**
>
> - Acknowledgement and appreciation
> - The work itself, the activities
> - Balance between work and personal life
> - Personal development and growth
> - Relationships with colleagues
> - Compensation (salary, benefits, etc)
> - An environment in which you can be successful, achieve goals
> - Responsibility and autonomy

Add to this list if you have other factors that are personally important to you.

Choose the top four things that are the most important to you. Then prioritize them from 1 to 4 (1 being the highest).

Now reflect upon your work situation and give each of your top four a score that is between 1 and 10 (1 is low). How do your motivation factors score in the current period of your life?

Are any of them scoring low, by your standards? (This is very subjective ... for me, a score of 6 already feels low.)

If yes, how could you increase this motivation factor by one or two points? What would the difference be for you between a score of 5 and a score of 7? What needs to happen or change?

Discuss your motivation factors with other colleagues, and especially with your manager. Think of ideas to increase any low scoring ones, and then take action. Work on trying to get all of your top four to higher levels.

As your scores go up, I guarantee you will experience increased energy levels, more satisfaction from your work and an enhanced overall feeling of well-being.

28. POSITIVE PEOPLE

The people you interact with have a huge impact on your life and energy. A popular statement made by many motivational speakers is that "You are the average of the people with whom you spend the most time". With regards to your energy, this has been proven to be true time after time in studies of recent years.

Whenever you interact with others who are either consciously or unknowingly negative, you will automatically absorb some of their negative energy. These are people who frequently focus on the less good things in their work and lives and cause you to do the same. They are often unwitting parasites who suck energy out of you.

When you spend time with people who are positive and optimistic, who know how to uplift their own spirits and work at 'becoming their best self', you inevitably feel and absorb some of their positive energy. You will be uplifted, will experience more happiness vibes and less stress. Which type of people are you hanging out with?

In terms of energy management, it's good to think about this question in the same way as you might think about what you eat and how you are keeping physically fit through exercise.

Which people are energizing to spend time with?

They don't have to be saints, living their lives in a perfectly harmonious positive and optimistic way. People who see the proverbial glass as half full instead of half empty are good to hang out with: they have a positive can-do attitude that inspires others; they provide you with motivation to move forwards to achieve your goals, encourage you to action changes you have decided to implement in your life.

You know who they are ... because after every interaction with them (face to face, telephone call, email, text message), you feel more energized.

HERE IS A SET OF ACTIONS TO HELP YOU WITH THIS PROCESS:

- Make a list of the people with whom you spend the most time

_____

_____

_____

- Write down their qualities. Would you classify them as positive people? Happy?

_____

_____

_____

- How do they interact with you? How do they affect you?
- Do you feel energized after interacting with them? Or the opposite?
- Do they support you, and make you feel like you have what it takes to achieve your goals?

Make an affirmative decision and take action to spend more time with the people who make you feel happy and energize you. People who make you laugh, who help you when you're in need.

These are the ones worth keeping close to you in your life. Everyone else is just passing through! This approach is a guaranteed formula to deliver more positive energy in all parts of your life. Try it, you'll be amazed at the results.

29. ENERGY LEVEL

I'm sure you know the feeling of having varying levels of energy at different times of the day ... it is fascinating to think about the reasons for this!

This is what I want to focus on: why your energy levels vary, and how can you better manage them.

I'm going to launch straight into the heart of this subject ... the importance of being aware of the amount of energy you have, of measuring it.

If I ask you, "how much energy do you feel you have at this very moment?" And I mean all four energy types (emotional, physical, mental and purpose), not just physical. What would your answer be, on a scale of 0-10? Give yourself a score of 10 if you feel you're buzzing like a live wire, 0 if you feel like you're just about to collapse in a heap.

I find the best way to do this is to briefly close your eyes, and feel what your level is.

I'm an 8.5 at the moment, how about you?

Say it out loud to yourself, and write it down.

Now I want you to think back to when you got out of bed this morning, what was your energy level then? Again, write it down, on a scale of 0-10.

And what was your energy score, say, two hours ago? Write this down too.

It's a fact of life that everybody's energy level goes up and down during the day, and it's an interesting exercise to ask yourself why.

What have you done, or what has happened to you to affect your energy level? Where and why did you lose energy? From what or whom did you get an energy boost?

By measuring your energy level at different times of the day – and then reflecting for a few moments – you'll start to get a much better understanding of what gives you energy, and what takes it away.

Then the next step is, as much as possible, try to more consistently focus on doing the things that give you extra energy. And try to reduce spending effort and time on the things that sap your energy.

THE SUGGESTED ENERGY ACTION IS:

Keep a log of your energy level on a daily basis, measure it at least four times a day. Each time write it down, and then reflect upon the differences that happened during your day.

Play with this concept. For example, measure your energy before you start a meeting, and then again immediately afterwards ... what happened?

Did the meeting give you energy or cost you energy? And why? What could you do differently next time?

30. TRY TO ENJOY EVERY MOMENT OF EVERY DAY

One of my philosophies in life is to *try* to enjoy every moment of every day.

I don't always succeed, not by a long way. But by frequently reminding myself to try, I often increase my enjoyment of the moment. And this automatically gives me an energy boost.

I consistently preach this to everybody I meet, time and time again. Because I'm 100% convinced that attitude of mind is the most powerful energizer there is.

A lot of the time people react with: "yeah, these are great words Richard, but bloody difficult to put into practice ... there are lots of things I have to do that I really don't enjoy."

And I ask: Why?!

Why are you living a lot of your relatively short life on this planet under dark clouds? What's the problem in trying to continually create blue skies? I emphasize the word **try**!

I don't know anybody who doesn't want to lead a long, happy, healthy and fulfilling life, do you?

No, of course not. We all want this sort of life.

One way to significantly enhance this is to adopt the following two attitudes:

- **Do what you enjoy!**
- **Enjoy what you do!**

To do what you enjoy means firstly understanding what you like, what you're good at, what gives you energy. And then finding ways to do more of these things.

To enjoy what you do means to constantly look for the positives ... even in situations that are boring, routine, difficult, sad and so on. Like everything in life, the more you practice, the better you become.

We all know the cliché, do you see the glass as half empty or half full? Well, here's a Zen saying you might not know: after my house burnt down, I could see the moon more clearly.

In almost everything in life, there's a positive aspect to be found.

AT THE RISK OF REPETITION, I SUGGEST THE FOLLOWING ENERGY ACTIONS:

- *Try* to enjoy every moment of every day, it's all in your hands and mind. You are in control
- Do what you enjoy, as much as possible
- And lastly, enjoy what you do, whatever it is you're doing, whatever the circumstances

31. 'YOU WORDS'

Did you have a nickname at school?

A nickname given to me by a friend was 'chopper', because of the hard tackles I made as a football centre-half. The image was of me chopping people's legs from under them! I didn't see myself this way, and I never injured people ... I was just very determined.

And 'determined' is most definitely a word I use to describe myself, a 'Me Word'.

If you had to describe yourself in just one word, the way you see yourself, what would this word be?

Spend a minute or two choosing this word before you read further.

Of course, like me and everybody else, you can't be described in one word, you have many different strong characteristics. I'm sure when you were trying to decide on one word, several other words passed through your mind.

Each one of these is probably one of your 'You Words'. Take a few moments to write down all of the words that floated through your mind. Now add more words to this list, try to make a set of 10 to 12 words.

FOR EXAMPLE, MY LIST OF 'ME WORDS' IS:

smiling	balanced	goal-driven
determined	positive	optimistic
passionate	disciplined	energetic
structured	can-do	relationship-oriented

Once you've made your 'You Words' list, take a long and hard look at each word, commit them to memory. Know that this set of words is the best description of you, as you see yourself. You are most definitely the person who knows you the best!

Keep this list on your smartphone and in other easily accessible places. Whenever you want a quick feel-good energy and self-esteem boost, have a look at your list of 'You Words'. They highlight the strong, good aspects of you ... know yourself to be this person.

PS: 'You Words' are excellent to weave into any introduction of your-self, and to add to your curriculum vitae.

32. WONDERFUL YOU

When you see your reflection in a mirror, how often do you really look at yourself? I don't mean just physically, but your whole being.

How do you see yourself, what sort of person are you? Are you comfortable and happy with who you are? Are you able to truly 'be yourself' most of the time? How often do you put on masks to pretend to be somebody you aren't? Or try to hide certain parts of the 'real you'?

Well that's a load of questions for you to think about. The point I want to make is this: the more you're able to be the true you, the happier and more successful you'll be in life.

When you're acting, pretending, trying to project an image of something you think you should be, instead of just being yourself ... it not only costs a huge amount of energy, it limits the impact of all of the fabulous things that are naturally yours.

'Being Authentic' has become a bit of a cliché during recent times, but forget the cliché. If you want to have more fun, happiness and success, it's absolutely essential to spend as much time as possible being you. To be able to do this, there are a couple of provisos:

- You need to feel reasonably happy with yourself ... know that you're a wonderful, unique human specimen, with lots of qualities and strengths, and some imperfections
- And it's important to stop worrying about what you think other people might think about you

This last point is especially tricky for many people, and it's certainly linked to the first point. Because when you're happy with yourself, you have more self-confidence, and then you're automatically less concerned what others think about you.

Here's an extra tip to help you.

Whenever you meet anybody and have a concern about what they might think about you, visualize them sitting on the toilet with their trousers around their ankles ... something they do at least once a day, just like you!

With this picture in your mind, you've created a level playing field. You can then more easily just be yourself.

THE SUGGESTED ENERGY ACTION IS:

- Make a conscious effort to spend all of today just being yourself, in all circumstances ... go for the 100%
- Repeat the process tomorrow, and the next day, and the day after ...

Enjoy being authentic, have fun being the wonderful YOU!

33. LAUGH YOUR HEAD OFF

You might have heard the expression "a day without laughter is a day not lived". But did you know that it's not only fun to share a good laugh, it increases your energy and can improve your health. It triggers physical and emotional changes in your body.

Laughter strengthens your immune system, creates a positive mood and diminishes pain. It brings your body into balance.

Humour has the power to inspire hope, to lighten your struggles, it connects people, and it helps you to be sharper and more focused.

This powerful resource is available to us all ... and best of all, it's free!

HERE ARE A FEW OF THE MANY SPECIFIC BENEFITS:

- Endorphins (our natural feel-good chemicals) are released, which increases positive energy
- Stress hormones are decreased and immune cells are increased, making you more resilient
- Negative emotions are stopped ... you can't feel angry, sad or anxious when you laugh
- Physical tension is reduced ... a good laugh can relax your muscles for up to 45 minutes
- You view situations more realistically, your perspective shifts

It's important to remember you were born to laugh, it's a natural part of life, you received this gift at birth. And you can rediscover this gift at any time in your life, by working on it ... just like you might exercise or go to the gym to work on your physical fitness.

How can you bring more laughter into your daily life? Start by blocking time in your agenda, to laugh and search for humour.

HERE ARE SOME TIPS AS TO HOW YOU CAN USE THIS 'LAUGHING TIME':

- Create a collection of short YouTube videos that make you laugh ... and watch one on a daily basis
- Look for funny stories on the internet
- Play fun games with children ... try to emulate them by letting go and releasing your inner child
- Do something silly
- Watch a comedy film or TV show
- Go to a comedy club with a few friends
- Spend time with people who make you laugh
- Write down amusing things that happen to you, and funny stories/jokes you read or hear ... and share them with others

Above all, don't take yourself and life too seriously. Laugh at yourself, at the mistakes you make, at embarrassing moments that happen to you.

The more you laugh each day, the less effort it will cost. It will become a natural response to see the funny side in all of your activities.

Start today, and make a conscious commitment to laugh your way through life.

34. ENERGIZING IMAGES

As humans, we are blessed with such powerful brains. One of the many magical things we all possess is the power of imagination. You can close your eyes and visualize things, see pictures in your mind, especially of people and events that have happened in the past.

When you allow positive uplifting images to enter your mind, these always have a positive impact on your emotional energy level and your feeling of well-being. By the way, the opposite is also true ... negative images negatively impact your energy!

Here is an easy way to immediately switch into a positive mood, anywhere, anytime.

Take an hour (more if necessary) to go through all of your digital photos. Pick out ones that, when you see them, instantly bring a smile to your face, and give you a strong fuzzy warm feeling. Photos of special moments, of family members and friends, of yourself ...

whichever grab you. Create a folder of 'Energizing Images' containing around 20-30 of your favourite, most energizing photos.

And then whenever you want to give yourself an instantaneous energy boost, open this folder and slowly look at each photo. Take the time to reflect upon each image, allow the positive memories and feelings related to the photo to flood into your system.

This is such a simple and yet hugely powerful way to increase your energy. Keep enjoying this process again, and again, and again.

35. AVOID YOUR PITFALLS

Booster 31 introduced the concept of 'You Words' – a list of 10 to 12 words that describe you and the way you see yourself. Revisit this list and choose the top four strongest words, the ones that always seem to be in the forefront. These will be characteristics that are prevalent in both your work and personal life, and they will have been prominent since your teenage years, if not before.

All of your 'You Words' are qualities that have a positive impact for you and those you interact with.

However, these strong descriptors can sometimes also have an undesired negative impact. This happens when you take a specific strong characteristic too far, when you use it excessively in a given situation, go 'over-the-top'. The behaviour that then occurs is called a 'pitfall'.

I'll explain this by using one of my top four words, 'Goal-driven'. It's a fabulous quality that has hugely helped me and others throughout my life, in making things happen.

Ask anybody who knows me: "What is one of Richard's characteristics/qualities that you admire?" Most people will say something like, "He makes things happen, is goal-driven, has a results orientation."

But sometimes I become obsessive with my Goal-driven attitude. I become blinkered about what really needs to happen. I become fanatical about achieving the goal at all costs, and I push others around me to do the same. And this going 'over-the-top' behaviour is disliked by those I'm interacting with. They become irritated, frustrated and generally react with a negative response.

So, when you slip into pitfalls, what was a good quality, a strength with positive impact, turns into a negative – this is always the end result. And instead of creating positive energy by using your top four strengths in an appropriate manner, when you are in your pitfalls, you generate negative energy.

I want you to look at each of your top four 'You Words' and reflect upon what the specific associated pitfall is for each one.

HERE ARE SOME EXAMPLES (QUALITY – PITFALL):

- Structured – Inflexible
- Helpfulness – Interference
- Flexibility – Inconsistency
- Independence – Individualist
- Modesty – Passiveness
- Decisiveness – Forcing
- Goal-driven – Pushy

When you have identified your top four pitfalls, try to observe the situations when you slip into them. Ask a couple of people with whom you spend a lot of time (e.g. family member, friend, colleague) to let you know when this happens.

Slowly but surely, you will begin to recognize when you are about to fall into one of your pitfalls and will be able to stop it from happening. By avoiding your pitfalls as much as possible, you will then increasingly experience only the positive impact and energy from your top four qualities.

36. TO BE OR NOT TO BE ...

... that is the question, said Hamlet in Shakespeare's famous play of the same name.

Well no offence intended to Mr. Shakespeare, but there is no question for me ...

I want 'to be'. Let me explain what I mean.

Do you make to-do lists, either in your head or noted somewhere, important things that need to be done sometime? I do, and I imagine you do too. Otherwise, with the many different things that you're busy with, you might forget some of them.

How do you feel when you've completed an item on your to-do lists? Maybe a short-lived sense of achievement, a feeling of relief?

Does your to-do list ever become empty? Of course not, you constantly add new things to it. And when you've 'ticked the box' for an item on your list, you start to focus on the next most important or time-critical one.

Working through your to-do list is a disciplined way of making sure the necessary things get done. But it doesn't give any real energy boost. In fact, to-do lists often make us feel stressed, over-challenged, even resentful.

I highly recommend that you make another type of list, in addition to the to-do one: your 'to-be' list. Because after all, you are a 'human being' not a 'human doing'!

To-be lists are focused on who you want to be as a person. They're not about trying to become somebody different, they're about being the authentic real you ... the qualities you would like to embody, the feelings you want to feel, the way you want to be in your life.

It's good to make to-be lists for the short, medium and long term.

When thinking about items for your long-term list, consider the following question: What would you like your family, friends, former colleagues to say about you at your funeral?

It may seem like a morbid way to think, but it will provide you with excellent input to understand who you really want to be in life.

For your short-/medium-term to-be list, think about how you would like to experience the coming days/weeks/months.

HERE ARE A FEW IDEAS:

I want to-be (more):
- healthy
- energized
- peaceful
- motivated
- focused
- caring
- loving

- reliable
- appreciative
- happy
- non-judgemental
- considerate
- forgiving
- supportive

Make your to-be lists, and then think about what you need to do in order to make progress in being who you want to be. Write down some actions and make your intentions actionable.

Review your to-be lists on a regular basis to reflect upon how you are living in line with these. When you lay down in bed, getting ready for a good sleep, is an ideal time to review your short-term list ... how did you live your day?

When you frequently focus on who and how you want to be, you will be infused with new positive energy every day. Remember, the quality of your life is determined by who you are, not by what you accomplish.

37. BE MORE PROACTIVE

One of the biggest drains of mental and emotional energy occurs when people are busy with things they can't influence. These things are a constant cause of frustration and irritation, because in general you can't do anything about them.

Proactive people focus on what they can influence, whereas reactive people often focus their energy on things beyond their control. Being proactive is more than just taking action or initiating things. It also means taking responsibility for our reactions to people or events. We are response-able and have response-ability ... because we have the ability to consciously choose how we respond to any situation.

As humans, we can think things through and don't need to be caught up in primal 'stimulus-response' patterns, in the way that animals are. To be proactive is to choose your response, rather than relying on instinctive reactions. People who don't consider their reactions are reactive and often blame others or things outside of themselves for what happens. They have a low level of response-ability.

We all get frustrated and irritated sometimes, this is normal. The important point is how you respond when this happens.

HERE IS A SIMPLE EXERCISE TO HELP YOU
INCREASE YOUR LEVEL OF RESPONSE-ABILITY,
TO BE MORE PROACTIVE:

- Make a list of things you have no control over, but that you spend time and energy thinking and talking about, maybe even complaining about. Some examples could be: the state of the economy; the clothes your children want to wear; attitudes in society; a company merger; the attitude of your colleagues; the way people drive their cars; the weather; etc. Your actual list will be personal to you
- Choose the three things from this list that frustrate or irritate you the most. The point is that there may be little you can do about these things because you can't influence them. Focusing on them may be a waste of time, and thus wasted energy, which once spent cannot be reused
- Review each one of the three things. Can you think of any possible actions you could take to change or influence it?

- If yes, are you prepared to invest the energy to try to change it, and accept the consequences?
- If yes, take action, try to change it
- If no, drop it, don't allow yourself to spend any more energy on it
- Repeat this exercise once per month

By focusing your energies more on things you can influence, your level of response-ability will increase, you will become more pro-active. And you will for sure experience reduced stress levels and increased positive energy.

38. RELEASE THE TENSION (1)

George Burns, the celebrated comedian, lived to be 100 years old ... and when he died in 2006, he was still working. One of his many famous quotes is: "If you ask me what the single most important key is to longevity, I would have to say it is avoiding worry, stress and tension. And if you didn't ask me, I'd still have to say it!"

In the fast-paced 24/7 constant-communication and interactive lifestyles that most people lead, it has become almost impossible to avoid some form of constant negative stress. This stress translates into tensions of all types in your body, and this in turn blocks energy ... physical, emotional and mental.

So, if negative stress is virtually unavoidable, how can you best deal with it?

First, it's essential to become aware of the tensions in your body. Stress-related tension shows up in various parts of the body, I call them 'stress traps'. The main ones are face, neck, shoulders, lungs/diaphragm and hips/legs.

This Booster focuses on the most important stress trap, your face. Why? Because the tension in your face has a massive impact on the tension you feel in the rest of your body. Releasing tension in your face sends messages to your brain that stimulate your whole system to relax.

Here are two exercises to help you achieve this.

FACE-STRETCHING

- Breathe slowly and deeply
- Stretch your facial muscles (there are 43 of them!) ... do this slowly and with forced tension
- Make sure you're moving all facial muscles: forehead, eyebrows, eyes, cheeks, jaw, lips, tongue
- For example, open your mouth as wide as possible, dropping your lower jaw to the extreme. Put the biggest possible forced smile on your face. Raise your eyebrows as high as possible. Stick your tongue out as far as possible. Screw your face up, make a grimace. It doesn't matter what you do, just contort your face to make expressions that stretch all muscles
- Do this exercise for one minute

FACE-MASSAGE

- Place the two first fingers of each hand on the sides of your face on your lower jawbone (at the level of your mouth, slightly closer to the ears than the mouth)
- Perform a massage, applying light pressure with the fingers and moving them in a circular fashion ... do this for 30 seconds
- Using the same two fingers of each hand, place them on your head temples, on the temporal bones (side of the head, behind the eyes, between the forehead and ears)
- Give your temporal bones a circular massage with your fingers ... do this for 30 seconds

At first, you might feel some discomfort afterwards. This is perfectly normal, it's a sign your facial muscles are waking up and that you're in contact with the depth of tension in your face.

When you practice these exercises at least twice per day, you will increasingly feel a sense of calmness and better balance. And you will for sure experience a more energized feeling, which will impact your physical, emotional and mental states.

Remember, when your face relaxes, everything relaxes ... not just inside you, but also the people with whom you interact.

39. RELEASE THE TENSION (2)

As mentioned in Booster 38, loads of energy gets trapped in your muscles and joints, in so-called 'stress traps'. Because it is such a major energy inhibitor, I'm dedicating another Booster to this subject.

Booster 38 focused on releasing tension in your face. This Booster helps you deal with stress traps in other parts of your body. For each area, I'll provide simple exercises to release tension and thus enhance your energy flow.

NECK
NECK ROLLS
- Tuck your chin into your chest, turn your head to the right and slowly roll it down and to the left, making a U-shape
- Then do the same thing in the reverse direction, from left to right
- Do this five times in each direction

CHIN RETRACTIONS
- Whilst standing, move your chin forward, then slowly pull it back by slightly tucking it into your throat. Make sure you keep your chin straight and parallel to the floor, not moving it up or down
- Repeat this ten times

NECK STRETCHES
- Bend your neck by moving your right ear towards your right shoulder. Place your right hand on the left temple and gently add a little pressure by pulling the head to the right. Hold this position for 30 seconds
- Now do the same exercise in the opposite direction
- Repeat the stretch on both sides three to five times

SHOULDER
SHOULDER ROLLS
- Stand up straight with your arms hanging loosely at your sides
- Roll your shoulders upwards, then back, then downwards, all in a flowing movement. Repeat this ten times
- Now roll your shoulders in the reverse direction, first upwards, then forwards, then down. Again, repeat this ten times

SHOULDER BLADES
- Whilst standing, bring your arms and hands behind your back, and clasp your hands together with the thumbs pointing downwards
- Slightly arch your upper back and move your shoulder blades gently towards each other

- Hold this position for ten seconds
- Now reverse the hand-clasp ... if your right thumb was on the outside of the clasp, change it so that the left thumb is on the outside
- Again, hold this position for ten seconds

SHOULDER ROTATION
- Standing with your back against a wall, stretch your arms out to the sides at shoulder-height. Bend your arms 90 degrees at the elbows, so that your hands face forwards and your biceps (upper arms) are in contact with the wall
- Keeping the elbows in the same position, turn your left arm upwards so that the back of your left hand touches the wall. Simultaneously turn your right arm downwards so that the palm of your right hand touches the wall
- Slowly keep switching, left arm up/right arm down, then left arm down/right arm up
- Do this exercise for 30 seconds

LUNGS/DIAPHRAGM
- The main way to release tension and extra energy in this area involves deep 'belly-breathing'. This is covered extensively in Booster 15

HIPS/LEGS
HIP STRETCH
- Sitting on a chair with a straight back, place your left ankle on your right knee
- Bend your body forwards until you feel a gentle stretch
- Maintain this position for one minute
- Reverse the position and repeat the exercise

RELAXED LEGS
- When people are sitting behind a desk or in meetings, they often cross their legs one over the other, or bend their legs backwards at the knee and cross their feet at the ankles. Both of these actions increase tension in the legs. The answer: uncross your legs and ankles and keep both feet firmly flat on the ground

Releasing tension in any part of your body will automatically enhance the flow of energy in your system. Try these exercises on a regular basis and I guarantee you will feel more energized.

40. MORE FOREPLAY

Take a couple of minutes to think about upcoming fun events that you've planned to happen during the next few months. Maybe a vacation, a musical concert, a theatre show, visiting friends, a night out, a work event, a course to develop yourself, a new experience ... anything that you're looking forward to. Make a list of these events.

Now look at each item on your list and spend a few moments thinking about each one, visualize it happening.

How do you feel after this exercise?

I would be surprised if you don't feel some extra positive energy, smiling on the inside and possibly with a smile on your face.

We all get positive energy from the anticipation of nice things we've planned for the near future. The happy energy you feel from anticipation is as real as the energy that comes from the actual experience.

Anticipating is not the same as fantasizing. Fantasizing is not based upon an actual thing that is going to happen, but on something which may or may not occur. Anticipation connects you to a future event that is going to happen, and you can begin to feel the actual experience of it happening.

Of course, it's important to have some fun events planned in your diary. If you don't already have a few, plan a couple today.

As one of these events, maybe include a totally new experience. Consider something that's been on your list of potential activities for a while. For example, a cooking course, dancing/singing/musical instrument lessons, a scuba diving course, a parachute jump. It doesn't have to be anything hugely adventurous, just something that excites you and you've been thinking about doing one day.

New experiences have been scientifically proven to be one of the best ways to energize and stimulate human beings.

The extra energy you get from the act of anticipation is just like foreplay in a sexual encounter. It strongly arouses many of your senses and releases lots of positive energy.

I highly recommend you have more foreplay.

41. 47-MINUTE MEETINGS

Most organizations have what I would call a meeting culture. People's agendas seem to be full of meetings, and tele-conference calls, that keep recurring on a frequent basis ... weekly, monthly and so on.

Normally nobody challenges these time- and energy-consuming activities and asks whether they could be done differently. We just keep going to them like 'lambs to the slaughter'!

I would be greatly surprised if you believe that every minute you spend in meetings or on calls is a good usage of your and everybody else's time. The vast majority of people feel that meetings and calls could be shorter, less frequent, possibly deleted completely. It's not only time that feels wasted, it also puts unnecessary demands upon your precious energy.

And when we do have meetings, why are they always scheduled for multiples of 30 minutes?

The simple reason is we've always done it this way. The old paper diaries drove us to start and finish meetings on the hour or half-hour, and Microsoft's Outlook pushes us in the same direction. Every time you arrange a meeting through Outlook, it automatically suggests a minimum 30-minute slot.

One of the bad consequences of this is you frequently find your agenda blocked with back-to-back meetings and activities, with no 'white space' in between.

It's almost impossible to finish a meeting or activity at, for example, 11:00, and then start the next one at 11:00 ... usually, you can't logistically do this. Worst of all, it leaves no time to have a personal debrief/reflection on what you were just doing, and no time to prepare for the next activity.

I want to encourage you to start pushing back, to try to change this approach.

One way for example is to arrange meetings, for which you are responsible, for 47 minutes ... or any other number of minutes that seems appropriate. And when you're invited to a meeting of 60 minutes, send a reply that you can only attend for 47 minutes.

This will for sure get a response, which might lead to further discussion to do things differently.

HERE IS A SUGGESTED LIST OF POSSIBLE ACTIONS
TO HELP BREAK THE MEETING CULTURE HABIT, AND
TO REDUCE TIME AND ENERGY SPENT IN MEETINGS:

- Don't accept all meeting invitations immediately.
  If you don't think you should attend, ask the organizer:
  Why is it important for me to be there? What's the
  value for me? What contribution is expected from me?
  Can somebody else attend instead of me?
- As mentioned above, schedule shorter meetings
  for 47 minutes, 19 minutes and so on ... adjust the
  Outlook invitation timeslot accordingly, and suggest
  this approach to others who organize meetings
- Demand an agenda for every meeting. No agenda,
  no meeting!
- Have 'standing-only' meetings with no chairs or
  tables available
- At the end of each meeting, ask for a Recap/Actions/
  Action-Owners/Deadlines. This should be the last
  point in almost every meeting ... and checking this list
  should be the first point in a subsequent meeting
- Request that all laptops, smartphones and the like
  be turned off and removed from the table (including
  in one on one meetings), unless they are needed to
  contribute to the meeting

Each of the ideas above has the potential to win back some time
for you, and will enable you to use your energies in more effective
and efficient ways. Try it, you will undoubtedly create positive waves
around you.

42. GROWTH AND CONTRIBUTION

We all have six basic needs. They are universal, apply to everybody and drive all human behaviour. They are what 'makes us tick'. These basic needs can be split into two groups: primal and purpose needs. The primal ones are:

- **Certainty** – the need for stability, reliability and security
- **Variety** – the need to be stimulated, to experience change and challenge
- **Significance** – the need to be recognized, to feel acknowledged and appreciated
- **Connection** – the need to feel connection with others, to love and be loved

As human beings, we try to meet these four primal needs every day of our lives. There is no conscious effort required, our desire and drive to satisfy these needs is automatic.

The purpose needs are:

- **Growth** – the need to develop, improve and grow, both in our capacities as well as in character
- **Contribution** – the need to give and make a contribution to those around you, to help others, to make a difference in the world no matter how big or small

These two purpose needs have a massive impact on your emotional and purpose energies. They determine whether you experience stable, long-lasting, positive energy or merely momentary pleasure, and so whether you feel fulfilled or unsatisfied.

I want to challenge you to think about how you can focus more on meeting your growth and contribution needs.

Let's first look at Growth.

Your Growth need has the potential to breathe life into all areas of your existence. You have an innate desire to develop physically, emotionally, mentally and purposefully.

It's important to understand that Growth is a journey, not a destination. It's not about achieving goals. It's an ongoing attitude that allows you to be yourself, to be authentic, with all of your imperfections. It's about continually reflecting upon what you've discovered and learned, and how you would like to grow further.

THINK ABOUT THE FOLLOWING QUESTIONS:
DURING THE LAST YEAR ...

- How, and in which areas of your life, have you grown?
- How have relationships with your loved ones, friends, colleagues and others developed?
- What have you learned, about life and how you want to live?
- In which areas of your life would you like to grow during the next 12 months?

Now let's look at your contribution need.

Contribution comes from a fundamental desire to have our lives mean something, to make a difference no matter how small. It might seem clichéd, but one of the ways to experience a great life is to give.

When you strip everything else away, life is really about creating meaning. And meaning doesn't come from what you achieve or get, it comes from what you contribute.

You can satisfy your contribution need by doing big things, or simply by doing small things like giving a smile to everybody you meet, helping people in need.

REFLECT UPON HOW YOU CONTRIBUTE:

- What do you consistently do every day to make other people's lives better?
- What did you specifically contribute to others during the previous month, week, day?
- How could you increase your contributions to add more value to the people around you, or the world in general?

When you concretely connect to your need for growth and contribution and take specific actions to satisfy both of them more, you will experience a huge increase in your emotional and purpose energies.

43. LIVE IN THE NOW

When you are alone – whether at home, at work or travelling – how much time do you spend ...

1. thinking about the future
2. thinking about the past
3. thinking about the present?

According to many studies on this subject, most people spend approximately 50% of their waking hours on numbers 1. and 2. ... on things other than what is happening at this moment, on what they are actually doing. In particular, the tendency is to be thinking about the future ... things that might happen or may never happen at all. This phenomenon is called 'mind-wandering'.

The same studies have shown that, when people are in uncontrolled mind-wandering mode, they are significantly less happy and less productive than when they are focused on the present.

This is because when it is roaming in an unplanned way, the mind is mainly generating noise and interference ... fears, worries, concerned projections of the future.

Of course, there are times when mind-wandering is beneficial, especially for creativity. Day-dreaming often leads to creative ideas or breakthroughs in both personal and work projects.

However, uncontrolled mind-wandering is not productive. It is so easy and natural to get caught up in your thoughts, and it is addictive. But it's not pleasant, in general not valuable and it is for sure not a good use of your mental energy.

As Mark Twain famously quoted: "I've had a lot of worries in my life, most of which never happened."

One of the keys to a balanced effective usage of your mental energy is to be able to pull yourself back into the 'now'.

HERE ARE SOME TIPS TO HELP YOU:

- Spend a few minutes 'belly-breathing' (see Booster 15)
- Do five minutes of physical exercise ... walk around, run-on-the-spot, stretch your arms and legs
- Step out of your thoughts and look at them objectively ... stop seeing your mind-wandering thoughts as 'the truth', because they are not!
- Talk to someone, call a friend ... this will break your chain of thoughts and help to put things into perspective
- Go outdoors for a few minutes, have a brief interaction with nature ... feel some leaves of a plant, stare at a tree, watch an animal in a field

All of these activities will help to pull you 'out of your head' and back into the present moment.

My suggestion is that you action one or more of the tips above several times per day, when you catch yourself in mind-wandering mode. Slowly but surely you will gain more control over your mind and will experience higher levels of focused mental energy.

44. POSITIVE JUDGEMENTALISM

The word 'judgemental' has a bad name, because most people use it in a negative sense. It's most commonly used to describe someone who expresses lots of opinions – usually harsh, critical or sarcastic ones – about other people.

The original meaning of the word is neutral, judgements can be either negative or positive.

Being positively judgemental creates positive energy in yourself and others. Being negatively judgemental does the exact opposite.

What's interesting is that human beings have a strong bias towards being negatively judgemental. When we are evaluating or judging people, we have a natural tendency to give negative stimuli more weight and attention than positive ones.

The bad news is that being negatively judgemental creates negative emotions like resentment, hostility, grievance and so forth. These emotions produce specific hormones in your body – including cortisol and adrenaline – which have an undesired negative impact on your Physical, Emotional and Mental Energies.

The good news is that you can successfully fight against your negativity bias ... by consciously giving more attention to the positive side of people when you judge them.

This doesn't mean you ignore other people's shortcomings. But you give more focus to their good qualities and strengths, to cancel out the distorted perception created by your negativity bias. This approach provides you with a more balanced and accurate evaluation.

ONE METHOD THAT ASSISTS WITH THIS PROCESS IS AS FOLLOWS:

- Before interacting with somebody, think about their qualities, strengths and some of their achievements and previous positive experiences you have had with them
- Then when you are talking with them, have this positive picture of the person in your head. Keep allowing their qualities and strengths to float around in your mind
- If you're interacting with someone for the first time, force yourself to only look for their positive aspects

When you do this, both your verbal and non-verbal communication will reflect the positive thoughts and pictures in your mind.

Positive judgementalism creates positive emotions and hugely helps to develop better relationships ... and it has a significant positive impact on your energy.

I highly recommend that you practice it a lot!

45. RESET YOUR LIMITING BELIEFS

Throughout your life you develop all sorts of beliefs. Some are valuable and functional, ones that empower you. Others are limiting. They prevent you from living a more fulfilled life and unleashing your full potential.

Your beliefs are basically assumptions or conditioned perceptions you make about yourself, about others and how you expect things to be in your world. Beliefs are feelings of certainty about what something means. They help you feel more certain about your future, making you feel safe and secure.

As such, you hold on to your beliefs, irrespective of whether or not they are actually helping you at this time in your life.

I want to focus on your limiting beliefs, the ones that aren't helping you and are holding back lots of your energy and potential. These are often created when you fail to question certain things on a regular basis. Over time these things start to seem like 'the truth' and they trap you into having a fixed view of the world.

But it's important to understand that beliefs are not facts. This has been known since ancient times. Here's a quote from Marcus Aurelius (Roman emperor 161-180 AD):

"Everything we hear is an opinion, not a fact. Everything we see is a perspective, not the truth."

Limiting beliefs affect what actions you take, which then affect what happens in your life and this in turn reinforces your limiting beliefs. It's a self-fulfilling prophecy in which you are your own worst enemy.

If you keep telling yourself the same 'old story' related to your limiting beliefs, this will continue to be 'your truth'. But when you rewrite your 'old story', you can significantly change your life and release a lot of empowering energy.

I want to challenge you to reset your limiting beliefs.

Close your eyes, take a few deep breaths and try to identify three limiting beliefs that have been producing unwanted or negative consequences in your life.

Open your eyes and write them down. Also list the negative consequences you've experienced as a result of these beliefs.

For example, three of my limiting beliefs used to be:

1. Life is hard work, and everything is my responsibility
2. If I want to succeed, everything I do needs to be perfect
3. I'm always too busy, I never have time to ...

Once you've noted three of your limiting beliefs and their negative consequences, cross them out. And now write a new empowering belief under each one.

For my three limiting beliefs above, I created the following new empowering beliefs:

The truth is ...

1. Life is fun, try to enjoy every moment of every day. Others need to take responsibility for their own things
2. Very few things in my life need to be perfect
3. I have plenty of time to do the things that are important to me. I need to make choices and prioritize

When you've completed this exercise, you will now have three new empowering beliefs to replace some of your limiting beliefs. Keep reminding yourself of these new beliefs, apply them multiple times every day.

By doing this, you will create your 'new story', which will help you to release massive amounts of positive energy and unleash more of your potential.

COMMON LIMITING BELIEFS

- I can't trust people because I've been betrayed before
- I can't pursue my dreams because I'm worried I might fail
- I can't do A because of B
- I don't have the willpower to ...
- I don't deserve love
- I don't want to get close to this person because I'm scared of rejection
- I don't have what it takes to succeed (skills, attitude, ...)
- I could never do that

46. SWEAT LIKE A HORSE

When I was growing up, if I ever said a phrase like "I'm quite sweaty" within earshot of my mum, she would say, "Richard, horses sweat ... ladies glow and men perspire".

Well, sorry mum, but I'm going to encourage my readers to frequently sweat, so that the drops of perspiration freely flow out of the pores all over their bodies!

Sweating can be embarrassing if you're at work, for example in a meeting or whilst giving a presentation. Particularly, the wet patches under your arms and beads of water on your forehead make you feel uncomfortable.

I'm not suggesting you should be sweating at work or when spending an evening out on the town. I want to motivate you to do some intensive exercise a few times a week, to really work up a sweat.

Why? Because it releases extra energy and has many excellent health benefits.

HERE ARE SOME OF THE KEY ONES. SWEATING:

- Boosts production of endorphins – exercising and prolonged sweating increases the level of feel-good hormones generated in your system
- Detoxifies your body – purposely induced sweating helps to flush the body of many toxic elements such as alcohol, salt, cholesterol and heavy metals
- Unclogs skin pores – which keeps your skin healthy and prevents blemishes and pimples
- Decreases chances of catching a cold or the flu – because sweat contains an antimicrobial peptide (dermcidin) that helps fight infections and germs
- Decreases stress and anxiety – sweating activates the so-called parasympathetic response in the body. This reduces stress hormones, thereby helping you to relax, to digest your food properly, and to recharge your physical energy

What are your favourite sweat-inducing exercises? Working out at the gym, cycling, fast-walking, running/jogging ...

Whichever ones work for you, set yourself a schedule to do some form of intensive exercise for at least 20 minutes, three times per week.

It will bring you all of the benefits listed above and will also give you a consistent energy boost every time.

47. LISTEN TO THE MUSIC

The power of music is undeniable. Amongst other things, it helps you tap into all sorts of emotions and stimulates the development of the brain. Listening to any kind of music helps build music-related pathways in the brain. And because music has a positive effect on our moods, it has been proven to enhance learning abilities.

It's also fascinating how music brings back memories. When you hear one of your favourite songs, you are often instinctively reminded of times and events that you associate with that song. It's almost like being able to travel back in time!

Listening to music is also a great way to give you different types of energy boosts. Rousing, high-energy music stimulates an extra energetic feeling, while quiet gentle music brings a sense of relaxation and calmness.

We all have different tastes in music ... which genres appeal to you most?

Make a list of your favourite songs/tracks for each of your preferred genres. Then on one of your digital music-playing devices, create a few playlists – one for each genre – each one containing five to ten tracks.

> **I HAVE FIVE SMALL PLAYLISTS THAT ARE SPECIFICALLY GEARED TO STIMULATE DIFFERENT TYPES OF ENERGY:**
>
> - High powerful energy (rock)
> - Relaxing calming energy (acoustic guitar)
> - Soothing energy (light classical)
> - Romantic energy (ballads)
> - Happy smiley energy (reggae)

Once you've created your playlists, whenever you want to give yourself a particular type of energy boost, listen to a few tracks from the specific playlist related to the desired energy.

An extra tip to boost your energy further is to really get in the flow by playing air-guitar (or drums, violin, or whatever) whilst listening to the music. Sing or hum along to the tune (see Booster 8), maybe even dance a little and move with the sounds.

'Listen to the music' and enjoy the energy that flows.

48. GOOD NIGHT, SLEEP TIGHT

A sure-fire way to recharge your physical, emotional and mental energies is to have a great night's sleep. For most people, an average of seven hours is ideal.

However, many of us don't find it easy to fall asleep quickly and often sleep lightly, sometimes in short blocks of two hours or less.

One of the reasons why this happens is because our brains are full of open loops ... things that we haven't closed or fully processed and are unfinished. When you lay down in bed, your brain focuses on these things and keeps you turning mental cycles. These thoughts don't just make it difficult to fall asleep, they linger in your mind and disturb your night's sleep.

I want to share a simple highly effective method to turn off this mental activity, to help you fall relatively quickly into a restful and recharging sleep.

The principle is to relive your day and look for all of the positive things you experienced during your waking hours, no matter how small.

These so-called 'positive moments' come in all shapes and sizes: something specific that happened to you or somebody else; a pleasant energizing conversation; something new or challenging you did; a moment you gave a compliment to somebody; or when you received a compliment.

THE METHOD WORKS LIKE THIS:

- As you lay in bed, preferably on your back, eyes closed, run a film of your entire day, starting from the moment you woke up
- While the film is playing, every time you come across something you really enjoyed, that gave you positive feelings, stop and focus on this 'positive moment'... savour the emotions that are associated with this thing
- Keep moving through your whole day in the same way, letting the film run until you hit another 'positive moment'
- When your mind starts to wander away from the film of your day (as it will), restart the process from the beginning, from the moment you awoke

- When you've managed to relive your entire day, then focus exclusively on all of your 'positive moments' ... revisit each one of them in the chronological sequence in which they happened
- If you struggle to identify a few 'positive moments' in the day that has just passed, rerun the film of your yesterday

For many people this works well the first time they try it. Others sometimes need to practice for a few nights before the benefits kick in.

If you keep practising this method, you will fall asleep quicker, your sleep will be deeper and you'll probably have some interesting and pleasant dreams.

I wish you a good night, sleep tight and sweet dreams.

49. BREAK THE RULES

From a young age, you learned that you must obey rules. Your parents, teachers, friends and others have constantly given you what they consider to be well-meaning advice, to help you navigate a smooth path through life.

Some of these rules are very useful, such as: "don't touch a hot oven"; "don't steal from other people"; "do unto others as you would have them do unto you"; "two wrongs don't make a right"; "when in Rome do as the Romans"; "drive within the speed limit".

These types of rules are not only useful, they are more than reasonable. Accept these as good ones to follow. However, there are probably many other rules you are following that are not useful to you. In fact, they are quite possibly holding you back in certain areas of your life, and they cost loads of energy to obey.

These rules are often created by society in general, your peer groups, bosses at work, or even yourself. Somewhere along the line you convinced yourself that you must follow certain rules, without questioning them ... if for no other reason than you see others following them.

I want you to make a list of as many of these rules as you can think of. Then review each one to decide whether or not you wish to continue following it.

TO STIMULATE YOUR THINKING, HERE ARE SOME RULES THAT I BELIEVE ARE GOOD TO BREAK:

- Avoid failure – Rubbish! People that truly succeed fail again and again in life. You learn and improve from failures, so start taking more risks
- Wait for the right moment – There is almost never a right or perfect moment to take action. Not to get fit and healthy, to quit your job and start your own business, to call somebody you've lost contact with and so on. Stop waiting, just do it!
- If you don't plan, then you are planning to fail – Not everything in life can be planned out perfectly. And most plans never work out as originally conceived. For some things it's enough to know in which direction you want to go. Then take the first steps
- Follow in other people's footsteps – No! Don't do what others before you have done. You are unique, map out your own path and then follow it

- Success is a good job earning a great salary –
  No it's not. Your success is whatever you decide it is.
  Happiness leads to success not vice versa (check
  out *The Happiness Advantage* by Shawn Achor)
- Always have an opinion – This hugely limits your
  ability to learn from others. Try listening at Level 4
  (see Booster 23)
- Good work speaks for itself – Most people won't
  know what you've done unless you tell them. Profile
  yourself more
- What other people think matters – No it doesn't.
  Don't trap yourself in constantly seeking other
  people's approval
- Give as good as you get – This is a recipe for poor
  relationships. You reap what you sow, so give freely
  and unconditionally

I'm sure you will think of many more un-useful rules that you are following. Break them and you'll experience a huge release of positive energy, a strong sense of liberation.

50. LIVE YOUR VALUES

Your personal values are the things you believe are most important in the way you live and work. They serve as an internal compass that guides you throughout life. They help you to determine priorities, to make decisions ... and thus they shape your life and character.

Your values also have a huge influence on your energy and the way you feel. When your words and actions are in line with your values, you feel good and life is usually great ... you are satisfied and content.

But when there is a mis-match between the way you are living and your values, you feel a strong sense of conflict, frustration and possibly unhappiness.

Values start to form in early childhood. Your parents, upbringing, education, friends, and experiences all contribute towards this formation process. Once formed, values are normally quite stable

... although they can change as your life evolves, particularly when life-changing events happen, such as if you start a family and have children.

So it's good from time to time to reflect upon your values, to check if they are still consistent with what is most important to you.

Do you know what your top five to ten personal values are?

Here is a process to help you identify or confirm them.

STEP 1
Think back through your (personal and work) life, identify the times when you were: the happiest; highly energized; most satisfied and fulfilled; really proud. Write them down.

STEP 2
What were you doing at these times? Which factors contributed to the feelings of being happy, energized, satisfied, proud? Make notes.

STEP 3
- Find a list of (50-200) personal values examples on the internet ... there are many to choose from, all very similar
- Reflect upon the things you noted in Steps 1 and 2. Why was/is each time and experience really important to you?
- Pick out words from the personal values examples list that match your thoughts on the importance of these times and experiences. This is your draft personal values list.

STEP 4

Reduce your set of draft personal values to a maximum of ten values. You can often group multiple values under one main Value. For example, I combine the values Independence/Freedom/Risk/Self-reliance/Uniqueness under one main value called Autonomy.

Once you have clarified your list of five to ten personal values, start to use them as a checklist for making decisions about the choices you are faced with in life.

Frequently review this list to check if you are living your life in accordance with your values.

Learn to trust and rely upon your values. When you truly 'live your values', you will experience higher levels of happiness, satisfaction and energy ... and much less conflict, frustration, stress and anxiety!

REFERENCES AND FURTHER READING

Throughout my life I have been extremely fortunate to be constantly energized and inspired by many people around me ... in particular my family, friends and clients.

I have also been hugely impacted by several recognized leaders in the field of personal development. Their websites, blogs and books are excellent resources for additional information and insights.

ENERGY INSPIRERS

Tony Robbins – www.tonyrobbins.com
Robin Sharma – www.robinsharma.com
Michael Neill – www.michaelneill.org
Stephen Covey – www.franklincovey.com
Eckhart Tolle – www.eckharttolle.com
Nic Askew – www.nicaskew.com
Richard Leider – www.richardleider.com

ABOUT THE AUTHOR

RICHARD MADDOCKS

From an early age I noticed that I had a huge amount of energy. It always fascinated me where this came from and why other people often seemed to have less. I quickly realized that my main purpose in life is to constantly share my energy and help others to have more.

For 25 years I was instrumental in successfully building and growing technology companies of various sizes. Then I decided if I was going to be true to my life purpose and passion, I needed to explicitly focus on helping people to unleash more of their potential.

In 2000, I subsequently quit my role as CEO of an international IT organization and shortly thereafter co-founded Communicum, an innovative people-development enterprise.

Since this time, I have been privileged to assist many thousands of professionals in enhancing their energy, self-awareness, leadership and authenticity. I have delivered hundreds of workshops and seminars for many leading global corporations, as well as medium and small enterprises around the world.

The combination of my extensive business experience and deep understanding of how to help people release their potential has provided me with lots of simple and powerful insights, especially relating to the four types of personal energy.

The Energy Book gives me the opportunity to share my knowledge, insights and passion with 'the world'.

ADDITIONAL RESOURCES + AUTHOR CONTACT DETAILS

For additional information and valuable energy boosting exercises, please visit **www.the-energybook.com**

Please contact Richard for more details about In-company Workshops, Conference or Seminar Speeches, Teambuilding and Facilitating:
maddocks@communicum.nl
linkedin.com/in/richardmaddocks

As an internationally recognized inspirational speaker and workshop leader, Personal Energy Management is a central theme in all of Richard Maddocks' work. His passion for helping individuals, teams and organizations to unleash their potential has enabled thousands of people to experience more fulfilment and impact in all parts of their lives. The resulting positive effect for companies means he is a trusted partner for many clients to stimulate enhanced business success and work satisfaction.